PRAISE FOR THE NEXT BIG THING IS REALLY SMALL

"*The Next Big Thing Is Really Small* is an easy-to-read, informational, and insightful introduction to the emerging field of nanotechnology. . . . It is a must-read for anyone wishing to understand and profit from this burgeoning industry."

— Josh Wolfe, managing partner, Lux Capital, and editor of the Forbes/Wolfe Nanotech Report

"The book is a turn-on if you want your appetite not only whetted but fertilized and nurtured. It is comprehensive and compelling, and makes a strong case for nanotechnology, its importance, and its rapidly emerging impact, and the rationale for the national initiative that is already under way."

— Arthur H. Guenther, former president, International Commission for Optics, and research professor, Center for High Technology Materials, University of New Mexico

"*The Next Big Thing Is Really Small* is a call to invest in your future. Jack Uldrich and Deb Newberry give business leaders—in fact anyone working at developing and marketing new products—a sense of the exciting possibilities and huge potential of nanotechnology. They outline the key trends and show how nanotech will have great impact even on businesses that for now seem only indirectly affected. But tomorrow's winners—those who will develop and bring to market what today seem like science fiction products—are going to have to start immediately, and Uldrich and Newberry point the way."

— Herb Goronkin, Ph.D., vice president and director, Physical Research Labs, Motorola Labs

"Nanotechnology is a broad set of capabilities that will directly revolutionize or indirectly disrupt almost every industry over time. Distilled from a timeline of coming innovations in nanotechnology, *The Next Big Thing Is Really Small* translates these scientific advances into pragmatic business advice for adapting to the waves of change."

— Steve Jurvetson, managing director, Draper Fisher Jurvetson

"Uldrich and Newberry deftly separate nano-hype from reality, providing a concise, accessible, and thoughtful overview of nanotech's industry-by-industry impact over the next decade. Invaluable to any business or investor who wants to cash in on the future."

— James K. Glassman, author of *The Secret Code of the Superior Investor* and host of www.TechCentralStation.com

"The authors have done a remarkable job of breaking down the complexity and scope of nanotechnology and describing its impact on common, everyday life with strategies for businesses that serve it."

— Paul L. Gourley, distinguished member of science staff, Sandia National Laboratories

THE NEXT BIG THING IS REALLY SMALL

HOW NANOTECHNOLOGY WILL CHANGE
THE FUTURE OF YOUR BUSINESS

JACK ULDRICH

WITH

DEB NEWBERRY

CROWN
BUSINESS
NEW YORK

Published by Crown Business, New York, New York.

Member of the Crown Publishing Group, a division of Random House, Inc.

www.randomhouse.com

CROWN BUSINESS is a trademark and the Rising Sun colophon is a registered trademark of Random House, Inc.

Printed in the United States of America

Library of Congress Cataloging-in-Publication Data

Uldrich, Jack
    The next big thing is really small: how nanotechnology will change
    the future of your business / Jack Uldrich with Deb Newberry.
    1. Nanotechnology. 2. Business planning. I. Newberry, Deb.
    II. Title.
T174.7 .U43   2002
338'.064—dc21   2002011622

ISBN 1-4000-4689-0

10 9 8 7 6 5 4 3 2

First Edition

To our parents, Mary Kaye and John
and Dorothea and Delbert, for their
constant encouragement

To our spouses, Cindy and Jerry, for
their unwavering support and love

To our children—Meghan & Sean and Jennen,
Nathan, & Adriane—for providing us with
the inspiration to work for a better future

NANO·TECH·NOL·O·GY \na-nō-tek-'nä-lə-jē\ *n* (1987): the art and science of manipulating and rearranging individual atoms and molecules to create useful materials, devices, and systems

CONTENTS

THE NEXT BIG THING IS REALLY SMALL

INTRODUCTION

"TODAY'S SCIENCE FICTION IS OFTEN TOMORROW'S
SCIENCE FACT."

—STEPHEN HAWKING

Imagine materials one hundred times stronger than steel but one-sixth the weight. Cheap, supersonic transportation. Computers millions of times more powerful and efficient than those that exist today. The development of a host of cancer-curing drugs. These are not the predictions of some wild-eyed futurist; rather, they are the matter-of-fact conclusions of a group of serious, well-respected scientists describing the potential of a new, emerging field of science: nanotechnology.

You might be tempted to dismiss such predictions as unlikely or impossible. Don't. Less than a decade before the Wright Brothers' 1903 flight, Lord Kelvin, president of the Royal Society, confidently announced that "heavier than air flying machines are impossible." In 1943, Thomas

Watson, chairman of IBM, famously said, "There is a world market for maybe five computers." Even the esteemed Albert Einstein was wrong when he said, "There is not the slightest indication [nuclear] energy will ever be obtainable." The science behind nanotechnology is real; it is here now; it is constantly evolving, expanding, and improving; and it *will* change the way we live.

Nanotechnology, by definition, is the willful manipulation of matter at the atomic level to create better and entirely new materials, devices, and systems. To understand what this means, consider the following: Coal and diamonds are constructed out of the same material, carbon atoms. The arrangement of those atoms, however, greatly transforms both how those materials can be used *and* their value. One is an inexpensive fuel source, and the other is suitable for an expensive engagement ring.

The point is that the molecular composition of matter . . . matters. If we can manipulate the atom, then the rules of the game for almost every product change. From the food we eat, to the clothes we wear, to the materials and products we manufacture, to the buildings we live and work in, to the cars and planes we use, to the composition of our very own bodies, everything around us consists of atoms and will be impacted by nanotechnology.

While the science of nanotechnology cannot yet rearrange the carbon atoms in coal to make diamonds, it is advancing rapidly and will be inundating the business world during the next few years—and for the foreseeable future. You may be tempted to wait until the buzz dies down before deciding how to integrate, implement, or incorporate it into your business, but don't make the mistake of thinking of nanotechnology as a futuristic, outlandish concept straight out of a *Star Trek* episode that you have *years* to prepare for. Even though it may sound far off at times, within the decade nanotech will have huge effects on many practical industries, including manufacturing, health care, energy, agriculture, communication, transportation, and electronics.

The reason is simple. The tools for manipulating matter are becoming increasingly sophisticated, and our improved knowledge and understanding of how atoms and molecules can be controlled is going to lead to significant improvements in existing materials and products. These developments, in turn, will lead to the design of entirely new products, new applications, and new markets. And the reality is that it will probably be sooner than later. Before 2010, the market for nanotechnology products and services is expected to reach $1 trillion in the U.S. economy and will require anywhere from 800,000 to two million new jobs.

This is why every major government in the world is now investing in nanotechnology and why the U.S. government alone has increased funding from $422 million in 2000 to a projected $710 million in 2003, according to the NanoBusiness Alliance. It is why major corporations are outspending government by a ratio of 2 to 1 and why venture capitalists are expected to increase their funding in nanotechnology fivefold by 2004. It is why a dozen universities have established multimillion-dollar nanotechnology centers since 2001 and why dozens more are expected to do the same in the years ahead.

Nanotechnology is going to be big. In fact, although it deals with the very small—a nanometer is $1/80,000^{th}$ the diameter of a human hair—it is going to be bigger than big. It is going to be huge. Nanotechnology will require you to rethink radically what your core business is, who your competitors are, what skills your workforce will need, how you train your employees, and how to conduct long-term strategic planning and think about the future.

Skeptical? In 2001, there were 180 patents dealing with nanotechnology. This is up from 45 in 1999 and up from zero just ten years ago. According to Richard Smalley, the 1996 Nobel Prize winner in Chemistry, "The impact of nanotechnology on the health, wealth and lives of people will be at least the equivalent of the combined influences of microelectronics, medical imaging, computer-aided engineering and man-made polymers in the twentieth century." Mike Roco, senior adviser for nanotechnology at the National Science Foundation, has said, "Because of nanotechnology, we will see more change in our civilization in the next thirty years than we did during all of the twentieth century."

Still skeptical? "The Nanotech Report," a study of nanotechnology that has a purchase price of $4,700, found that the term *nanotechnology* was mentioned in professional articles and journals 1,800 times in 2000. This figure is comparable to the number of times *Internet* was cited in the early 1990s, before the Internet exploded and changed the face of how business operates.

This may sound like a lot of hype—and there will undoubtedly be a good deal of "nanomania" in the years ahead (much of it caused by the popular press, which will confuse nanotechnologies that are just around the corner with the highly speculative or the very long-term potential of nanotech)—but there is also very serious and solid science behind nanotechnology. Which might explain why in 2001 *BusinessWeek* named it one of their Ten Technologies to Watch and why *Red Herring, Scientific American, Forbes, Science,* and *Technology Review* have all dedicated cover issues to the subject since June 2001.

Unlike the Internet, however, which applied a new technology to many old processes and businesses, nanotechnology is about making entirely new materials, devices, and systems as well as making existing products faster, stronger, and better.

High barriers to entry in the form of large start-up costs, a deep knowledge base, and a strong intellectual-property portfolio also distinguish it from the Internet and make it extremely unlikely that a slew of former lawyers and marketing executives will be quitting their jobs (as many did during the dot-com craze) to start their own "nano" companies. In fact, you will be hard-pressed to find a nanotechnology company that does not have a scientist as either its founder or CEO. The bottom line is that there is real weight behind the buzz surrounding nanotech. Still, the alluring buzz may mislead those seeking instant gratification or expecting the world to change overnight. Technology changes rapidly. People do not.

This is not to say that nanotechnology is far-off, fuzzy, futuristic technology. It is not. It has already established a beachhead in the economy. The clothing industry is just now starting to feel the effects of nanotech. Eddie Bauer, for example, is currently using embedded nanoparticles to create stain-repellent khakis. This seemingly simple innovation will impact not only khaki-wearers, but dry cleaners, who will find their business declining; detergent makers, who will find less of their product moving off the shelves; and stain-removal makers, who will experience a sharp decrease in customers. This modest, fairly low-tech application of nanotechnology is just the small tip of a vast iceberg—an iceberg that threatens to sink even the "unsinkable" companies.

In late 2003, the flat panel display market (which supports the TV and computer industries) and toy industry will be introduced to nanotechnology. By 2005, the $100 billion computer-memory market will feel its cold, hard impact. Between the years 2006–2008, nanotechnology-enabled advances will reinvent the automotive and aerospace industries. And by 2013 (perhaps even sooner), the health-care industry will be on the verge of revolutionary change. Beyond that, the concept that nanotech will fundamentally alter almost everything around us—including our perception of ourselves—will be very real.

Whether you are the CEO of a multibillion-dollar semiconductor company, a heart surgeon, an automobile repair shop manager, a drug company representative, a psychiatrist, the division manager of a multimillion-dollar paint company, or even a house painter, nanotechnology is going to impact you.

The scientific breakthrough of 2001 was the construction of the first molecular-scale circuit. This advancement in the field of nanotech will usher in the post-silicon generation of electronics. Of course, the industry will go through an evolutionary phase of many years. But it is clear that twenty-five years from now processors and electronic devices will be radically different from what we know now—because of nanotechnology.

Medical advances in nanotechnology are on the threshold of being able to locate and destroy cholesterol molecules on demand. If successful, not only will the need for the number of heart surgeons decrease, but businesses that rely on supplying a cure or treatment for heart disease will be replaced by a technology that prevents the problem from occurring in the first place. Similarly, if depression is found to be molecular in nature and nano-technology, as believed, can assist in identifying the responsible molecules and help bind new drugs to those molecules to prevent depression, then a number of psychiatrists who treat patients for the disease, as well as Eli Lilly, the maker of the antidepressant drug Prozac, might also find that nanotechnology is eroding their business.

In 2001, Toyota Corporation introduced a new bumper made of unique nanocomposites that are 60 percent lighter than the material in existing bumpers and twice as resistant to denting and scratching. As more car parts are manufactured out of nanocomposites, your local car repair shop, like the corner grocery store of an earlier generation, might fade away. The impact will not, however, be limited to car repairmen. Fewer insurance adjustors will be required as the number of small claims decrease, and insurance companies, which rely on the revenue from automobile insurance, might need to rethink some of the basic assumptions underlying their business model. Like the carriage industry and chimney sweep of the nineteenth century, many industries and service-providers are likely to become icons of outdated products from an earlier era as a result of nanotech.

In the words of Richard Feynman, the man who first spoke about the possibility of manipulating matter at the atomic scale, nanotechnology is "a development which I think cannot be avoided." While it can't be avoided, the disruptive nature of nanotech can be anticipated, and those expecting its arrival can better prepare themselves for the massive change that is coming and, quite possibly, position themselves to take advantage of the opportunities that will inevitably arise from this new technology.

In this book, we will introduce you to the emerging and exciting field of nanotechnology and explain what it is, how you should think about it, how you can begin preparing for its imminent arrival, and what it might mean—

today and in the next ten years—for a variety of industries and industrial sectors.

For while it is impossible to predict the future accurately, the one thing we do know is that the future favors the prepared mind. We hope to prepare you for what will unquestionably be a very exciting future.

CHAPTER ONE

Nanotechnology: The Next Frontier

"NANOTECHNOLOGY HAS GIVEN US THE TOOLS . . .
TO PLAY WITH THE ULTIMATE TOY BOX OF NATURE—
ATOMS AND MOLECULES. EVERYTHING IS MADE
FROM IT. . . . THE POSSIBILITIES TO CREATE NEW
THINGS APPEAR LIMITLESS."

—HORST STORMER, NOBEL LAUREATE

On November 9, 1989, a new era dawned. The event that ushered in this era had nothing to do with the historic collapse of the Berlin Wall. Instead, the momentous event took place in the quiet confines of IBM's Almaden Research Center in San Jose, California.

Nearly fourteen years later, the date is still not accorded much significance. Future historians will, however, likely look back and use the November day to denote the official beginning of the Nanotechnology Age. For it was on that day that two IBM scientists, Don Eigler and Erhard Schweizer, purposely manipulated individual atoms to build a structure, a simple IBM logo. What made the logo so special was that it was created out of only thirty-five xenon atoms. For comparative purposes, the logo could fit 350 million times in an area the size of the period at the end of this sentence.

Eigler and Schweizer had broken the final barrier between humans and nature's most fundamental building block—the atom. And just as Wilbur and Orville Wright's short twelve-second flight was a precursor to landing on the moon, so too will Eigler and Schweizer's actions be precursors to tomorrow's fantastic journeys. Like the previous ages before it, the Nanotechnology Age began quietly. And just like the Stone, Bronze, Iron, and Silicon Ages, this new age will forever revolutionize the world. What will set the Nanotechnology Age apart will be the rate of change and the speed with which it will impact the world. Sixty-six years separated the events at Kitty Hawk, North Carolina, from the Apollo moon landing, but significantly less time will likely separate that day in 1989 from self-repairing materials, computers a million times more powerful than those of today, and biocompatible replacements for body parts (all three of which—and more—are under development).

If these things sound farfetched, ask someone born in 1960 if he thought his great-grandfather, who had grown up around the turn of the twentieth century—when 25 percent of all people were employed in agriculture and the average life expectancy was forty-seven years—could have envisioned that one hundred years later less than 1 percent of the population would work on farms and the average life expectancy would increase thirty years to seventy-seven. Could his grandfather's generation—makers of ENIAC, the world's first computer (which cost $4.7 million when it was built in 1946 and occupied an entire floor of a building)—have imagined that fifty years later an electronic greeting card would carry a comparable amount of computing power, cost less than a dollar, and be discarded by its recipient after playing a rendition of "Happy Birthday"? Or could his mother, who learned of DNA in high school, believe that in less than thirty years the entire human genome would be mapped and that people would seriously be debating the cloning of humans?

Your challenge will far exceed the technological challenges that previous generations faced, for two reasons. One, nanotechnology will impact almost every segment of society, and two, it will arrive—and already is arriving—much more rapidly than previous scientific advances.

It has been said that the only constant is change itself. From a business perspective, that is certainly true. Of the Fortune 500 companies in 1993, fewer than half still existed in 2002. The problem, which most people fail to grasp, is not that things will change. We all expect change. The problem, rather, is that the rate of change is not constant. Change is accelerating, and the technological developments are not moving linearly but exponentially. (The doubling of computing power every eighteen months, known as Moore's First Law, is one of the more commonly cited examples of such change.)

The situation is further complicated because seemingly separate and unrelated areas of science are now beginning to merge. Developments in one area of nanotechnology are fueling developments in another field, which in turn are contributing to developments in yet other fields. Consider the following: Material scientists are now developing new materials with enhanced electronic properties. These new materials will allow for the creation of faster computers. These faster computers will be used to generate more sophisticated computer simulation software, which in turn will be used to design even better materials. These new materials will then be turned around and used to build the next generation of ever-faster computers. The process thus continually repeats itself in an ever-shorter time frame. In addition to the creation of new materials, better software programs, and faster computers, these changes will also result in entirely new products, applications, and markets. Thus it is possible that the list of Fortune 500 companies a decade from now may be radically different from today's.

Over the next ten years, the fields of chemistry, physics, material sciences, biology, and computational sciences will converge in a way that will define nanotechnology and impact almost every industry, including computers, semiconductors, pharmaceuticals, defense, health care, communications, transportation, energy, environmental sciences, entertainment, chemicals, and manufacturing. Previously distinct disciplines will also combine: medicine and engineering, law and science, art and physics, etc. This merging will result in developments that are not simply evolutionary; they will be revolutionary. You need to be ready for them.

WHAT IS NANOTECHNOLOGY?

Nanotechnology is, broadly speaking, the art and science of manipulating and rearranging individual atoms and molecules to create useful materials, devices, and systems.

The term *nano* (derived from the Greek *nanos,* meaning dwarf) refers to one-billionth of something. Thus one nanometer is one-billionth of a meter, which is approximately the width of ten hydrogen atoms. For visualization purposes, the width of the dot above the letter "i" in this sentence is approximately one million nanometers. If that doesn't work for you, consider that one nanometer is to an inch what one inch is to approximately 16,000 miles. Or if each character of the alphabet could be printed at a height of ten nanometers, the entire *Encyclopaedia Britannica* (all 30,000 pages of dense print) could be replicated on the head of a common pin. Figure 1.1 gives some standard objects and their sizes in nanometers.

A key ingredient in understanding nanotechnology is realizing precisely what it is and what it isn't. When we refer to nanotech in this book, we are talking about research and technology development in the length scale of .1 nanometers to 100 nanometers to create unique structures, devices, and systems. In many instances the actual structures, devices, and systems will be much larger, but they will be classified as nanotechnology due to the fact that they will either be created at the nanoscale or nanotechnology will enable them to perform new and/or improved functions.

This broad definition encompasses two very important categories: nanomeasurement and nanomanipulation. The first, nanomeasurement, has largely been agreed by the scientific community to apply to only those things ranging in size from .1 nanometers (the size of a hydrogen atom) to 100 nanometers (the size of a virus). The rationale for choosing this size range is not merely a bureaucratic technicality. Many materials, once they are individually reduced below 100 nanometers, begin displaying a set of unique characteristics based on quantum mechanical forces that are exhibited at the

LESS THAN A NANOMETER
Individual atoms are up
to a few angstroms, or
up to a few tenths of a
nanometer, in diameter.

NANOMETER
Ten shoulder-to-shoulder
hydrogen atoms (balls in
center) span 1 nanometer.
DNA molecules are about
2.5 nanometers wide.

THOUSANDS OF NANOMETERS
Biological cells, like these
red blood cells, have diameters
in the range of thousands of
nanometers.

A MILLION NANOMETERS
The pinhead sized patch
of this thumb (black circle)
is a million nanometers across.

BILLIONS OF NANOMETERS
A two-meter-tall male is
two billion nanometers tall.

Figure 1.1 A nanometer is *very* small.

atomic level. Due to these quantum mechanical effects, materials may become more conducting, be able to transfer heat better, or have modified mechanical properties.

By using this definition, we will exclude some things that others now try to define as nanotechnology. For example, many items, such as Intel's latest semiconductor chip, which has transistors as narrow as 130 nanometers, can now be measured at a scale close to 100 nanometers. Most such advances, however, are the result of miniaturization using the same approach or process. For these advances to be truly representative of nanotech, they would either have to be manufactured, with a nanomaterial that enhanced the physical property of the product, or, alternately, assembled at the molecular level.

Another area that should be distinguished from nanotech is a class of miniaturized systems called MEMS (Micro Electrical Mechanical Systems). These tiny mechanical systems, which are the basis of a multi-billion dollar industry, use processes similar to those used for making semiconductors to manufacture devices like gears, pumps, and cantilevers. (Think of MEMS as traditional manufacturing only at a micro-sized scale.)

The distinction between nanomeasurement above and below 100 nanometers is very important because it has already become trendy in some business circles to affix the term *nano* to a company's name. But beware: Not all "nano" companies are created equal. Just because a company can measure some component of its business in nanometers does not mean that it is necessarily a nanotechnology company. (This does not mean, however, that the company's product is not viable or that the company is not a threat to your business. The business world will continue to be populated with many successful non-nanotechnology companies capitalizing on the commercialization of this new field, although few of these will evade nanotechnology's implications.) In fact, chemists and biologists have been dealing with and measuring things in the nano-range for decades—but they are only now beginning to learn the art and science of manipulating those things.

The other aspect of nanotechnology, the truly exciting side, is nanomanipulation, or building things from the bottom up, atom by atom. Nanomanipulation can be classified into two categories: nanofabrication and self-assembly. Nanofabrication (also called nanoscale engineering) refers to the actual atomically precise sculpting or building, with man-made tools, of products, structures, and processes. Self-assembly, on the other hand, is the process of atoms and molecules adhering in a self-regulated fashion, in which specific atoms and molecules bind to one another based on their size, shape, composition, or chemical properties. A tree constructing itself out of the surrounding molecules in the air, water, and dirt is an example, from Mother Nature, of self-assembly.

The distinction between nanofabrication and self-assembly can be more clearly illustrated using the computer chip as an example. Numerous companies, including Intel, IBM, and Hewlett-Packard, are working with carbon nanotubes in the hope that the thin tubes (1.4 nanometers in diameter, resembling a rolled tube of chicken wire) can be fabricated, integrated onto existing silicon chips, and used to make computers run much faster. (This technology will be discussed in greater detail in chapter six.) If successful—if carbon nanotubes can be used in an integrated circuit—this will undoubtedly be a legitimate business accomplishment, lead to more powerful computers, generate new business, and bring those companies (and the entire industry) into the nanotech arena.

On the other hand, numerous academic researchers as well as at least two commercial start-ups (Nanosys, Inc. and ZettaCore) are also constructing circuits by getting individual molecules to connect automatically in a prescribed pattern (self-assembly). If they pull this off and build a circuit from the molecule up, it will lead to vastly more powerful computers and entirely new products, applications, and commercial markets. In short, it will represent *revolutionary* change. The smart money is on this technology because a hundredfold reduction in size is actually the equivalent to a potential 10,000-fold increase in computing power, because the entire area of circuit is reduced one hundred times on both sides. Such an immensely more powerful computer will make real-time voice translation seem like child's play—so much so that the United Nations would need significantly fewer interpreters, and the travel and vacation industries would likely undergo some change as people became more likely to visit more and different destinations because language would no longer be a barrier. (Other nanotechnology-enabled advances in the areas of transportation and sensors will likely alleviate other barriers to foreign travel—such as cost and security concerns—and will also affect the travel industry.)

To paraphrase Clayton Christensen, author of *The Innovator's Dilemma,* whoever can commercially produce molecular circuits at a scalable level will have created a disruptive technology (one that can render billion-dollar industries obsolete). When a disruptive technology comes along, everyone—including business leaders—goes back to zero. Yesterday's accomplishments and achievements, no matter how big or profitable, will mean little. Just look at the above example of the molecular computer. It will require a completely different support infrastructure—software makers and chip manufacturers must adjust their products accordingly—and end-user applications will blossom as people and businesses find new uses for superpowerful, supersmall (and potentially supercheap) computers. For instance, if chips become small enough, suddenly the idea of tiny computers embedded in your clothing that can monitor your health no longer sounds so futuristic—or at least no more futuristic than the makers of ENIAC trying to envision a computer so small, so cheap, and so powerful that it could be used in a greeting card.

WHY IS NANOTECHNOLOGY IMPORTANT?

The nanometer is that magical point on the scale where man-made tools can begin to manipulate individual atoms and molecules. Everything from strength and electrical conductivity to optical, magnetic, and thermal properties has the potential to be modified based on the atomic structure and combination of the material being used. Therefore, by selectively arranging the material's atoms, everything from metals, ceramics, polymers, and semiconductors to glass and composites can be constructed for novel performance. In the words of Horst Stormer, this means that "the possibility to create new things is . . . limitless."

Think of it this way: If you blew up a household globe to the size of the earth, individual atoms would become visible. They would be approximately the size of grapes. These grapes can be manipulated and rearranged to create much more than a globe. They can be rearranged in such a manner so as to manufacture grape juice or even the equivalent of a 1989 bottle of Château Mouton-Rothschild Bordeaux. Materials and things that were once the realm of science fiction are now simply science.

In the past, man has simply taken the material that the earth has provided—wood, stones, ore, etc.—and found useful and creative applications for them, from the first spear to today's most advanced microchip. With some modification, these materials have allowed explorers to travel farther, skyscrapers to ascend higher, and submarines to dive deeper; but they are mere precursors to the new material age. In the future, applications will be conceived and entirely new materials will be created at the atomic level.

The reverse ordering of this process is a paradigm shift of historic proportions: The implications for the $460 billion global plastics industry, the $57 billion U.S. steel industry, and the $27 billion glass industry alone are staggering. Rather than limiting products to the specifications of the materials provided by suppliers, customers will be able to demand specifications to meet the needs of their product.

In 1886, there was only one type of Coca-Cola. It wasn't until 1982 that diet Coke was introduced. Since that time, caffeine-free Coke, Cherry Coke, diet Cherry Coke, caffeine-free diet Coke, diet Coke with a lemon twist, and most recently Vanilla Coke have been introduced. These advances, like the advances in a variety of fields, have provided customers with greater choice and more options. But the customer is still limited by the constraints of the producer.

What if, however, the customer no longer had to choose from a catalogue of existing materials but could instead tell the supplier exactly what she needed in a material? What if she could place an order with Coca-Cola for a lightly sugared, moderately carbonated, heavily caffeinated cola with precise doses of cherry, lemon, and lime without sacrificing the benefits of one trait (say, taste) to achieve the benefits of another (say, lower calories)? This is the potential of nanotechnology.

By managing and manipulating the composition and combination of atoms, metals can be made stronger and lighter, ceramics more flexible, and plastics more conductive. By combining or growing materials at different sizes (in the nanoscale region), even physical properties such as color and fluorescence can be modified. This will lead to longer-lasting lipsticks and mascaras with never-before-seen colors that will reshape the $18 billion cosmetics industry. The transparency of nanoparticles can also be modified. In fact, nanoparticles that are smaller than the wavelength of light are now being used in sunscreens so they can be applied transparently. Gone are the days of lifeguards wearing embarrassingly copious amounts of white cream on their noses.

Nanotechnology also holds the promise of combining organic materials like glass (which is usually hard and brittle) with softer inorganic materials. Suddenly a big flat panel display for a foldable computer is possible. If you combine this application with the earlier example of vastly more powerful computing power, the ramifications for the $550 billion global electronics market come into perspective.

THE BIG BENEFIT OF BEING TINY

In addition to exhibiting new properties at the nanoscale, the very size of the nanoparticles, nanocrystals, nanostructures, and nanomaterials imbues them with advantages. The first is that because they are so small, nanoscale materials have more of their atoms in contact with a surface. One pound of table salt, if spread across a table, would cover twenty-five square feet. One pound of the same table salt, if reduced to the nanometer, would cover five and a half acres. To understand, picture a grape. It occupies a certain amount of space on a table. If squished, it covers considerably more. This might sound unimportant, but it is significant, especially for the $30 billion catalyst market. (Catalysts increase the yield or efficiency of a process.)

An easier way to think about this is to picture your morning coffee. By grinding coffee beans into smaller particles, more of the bean is exposed to the water. This leads to fuller, richer-tasting coffee. In this way, a smaller bean particle is a better catalyst to creating good coffee. Moreover, because more of each bean is exposed to water, you use fewer beans, creating a more efficient process and saving money.

Now just imagine that you can tailor your coffee to your specific need. In the morning, you may need a lot of caffeine, whereas in the late afternoon or late in the evening, after a good dessert, you might want a sweet decaf. Further imagine that you could tailor your coffee not just to these needs but everything in between (and not just for you but for your whole family), and you begin to understand the potential of nanoparticles in the area of catalysis.

The small size of nanoparticles also makes them important for the pharmaceutical industry. Unlike their many micro-sized particle cousins, many nanoparticles are undetectable by the body's antibody system, meaning that the body does not reject the nano-sized drug as often. Similarly, unlike many micro-sized particles, nanoparticles are water-soluble. This means that the body can more easily digest the drug and reduces the likelihood of nasty side effects. (Just listen to all the disclaimers at the ends of commercials for today's drugs: "May induce dizziness, vomiting, . . ." These side effects are often attributed to the large particles of many drugs.) Further, nanoparticles' small size allows them to reach places that other particles or devices simply can't. Considering that many cells are in the range of thousands of nanometers in size, certain nanoparticles are small enough to penetrate the membrane of cells. Nanoparticles can also have modified surfaces to attach to receptor sites on the cell or to specific protein molecules in the cell. And it is this specific application that so excites cancer researchers, who understand nanotechnology's potential to deliver drugs to diseased cells.

To understand further the scale at which nanotechnology operates, consider that TheraFuse, Inc., a Vista, California start-up, is employing carbon nanotubes that are so slender that they can penetrate the skin without pain. The company is using the carbon nanotubes on patches that draw and test the blood of diabetics and administer glucose as needed.

NATURE'S YARDSTICK

Nanotechnology is also significant because molecular biology works at the nanoscale level. Thus, only by applying nanoscale science will we gain a deeper understanding of how our bodies—and the world around us—truly work.

With nanotech, man's ability first to see, then understand, and finally operate at the nanoscale all become feasible. For example, if we can understand why the molecular composition of bones deteriorates, then a remedy for osteoporosis becomes possible. If we can understand how the AIDS virus alters genes, we can move closer to a cure for this often deadly disease. The impact on the $180 billion pharmaceutical industry alone will be enormous, to mention nothing of the improvement in our quality of life.

Molecules that affect our bodies are already the basis of billions of dollars of commerce. From the molecular composition of caffeine that drives the coffee market to the molecules that make up ethyl alcohol and fuel the liquor industry, businesses from Starbucks to Miller Beer will be impacted by scientists' understanding of how molecules affect human behavior.

Many medical professionals believe depression, obesity, Alzheimer's, and a host of other ailments—both large and small—are molecular in nature, as opposed to genetic. If true, and if just a few of the government and academic researchers or start-up companies involved in this nanotechnology research are successful, how we view our health and how we practice medicine in the future will forever change. The $1.7 trillion health-care industry will be turned on its head. Everyone from the federal government's administrators of Social Security (who will have to adjust their actuarial tables to account for longer life expectancy) to the executives of the $90 billion U.S. insurance industry (who will have to pay for new treatments) will be impacted.

Consider how we treat cancer. Today's method of blasting radiation at regions of the body and, in the process, killing both cancerous and noncancerous cells will seem as crude to our children as the practice of a lobotomy for treating schizophrenia is to us. Why, our children will ask, was it necessary to poison the good cells as well as the bad? Which is precisely the question leading researchers at universities, government labs, and corporations are asking themselves. Many are approaching workable answers.

GREEN PRECISION

Many materials today work at a less than optimal performance level because the manufactured composite material out of which they are built contains defects. These defects can lead to material stress and ultimately failure, which, if they occur in an airplane at thirty thousand feet or within a building during an earthquake, can be devastating. At the nanoscale, however, materials can be made close to perfection, and this reduces the number of defects. That is, if a part is supposed to be exactly 100 atoms, it will be 100 atoms, not 99 atoms or 101 atoms. Also, when more than one type of atom is used, the ratio of atoms can be precisely controlled. This atomic precision significantly enhances quality and reliability.

Furthermore, because nanotechnology uses only those atoms that it requires, it is very efficient and clean. Unlike many of today's manufacturing processes that use complicated and unnecessary chemicals and solvents to synthesize materials and create new products, nanotechnology uses only what it absolutely needs. Nanotechnology is the ultimate in "green" manufacturing.

Consider the earlier example of the tree. Within the genes of a simple seed is contained the entire instruction manual necessary to build a tree. Then, using only the atoms and molecules from the surrounding dirt, water, and air and energy from the sun, leaves, bark, roots, etc. are formed. This example of self-assembly is very instructive because if Mother Nature can create something without creating any waste, it should just be a matter of time before molecular biologists working in partnership with chemical engineers and computational scientists begin to create products without unnecessary steps, unnecessary materials, or harmful chemicals.

WHY NOW?

In late 1959, Richard Feynman, later a Nobel Laureate in Physics, gave a lecture titled "There's Plenty of Room at the Bottom." In his talk, which is now famous in nanotechnology lore, Feynman said, "The principles of physics, as far I can see, do not speak against the possibility of maneuvering things atom by atom." Forty-four years later, his vision is on the verge of realization. The reason, like the vision of nanotech itself, was laid out by Feynman when he said, "The problems of chemistry and biology can be greatly helped if our ability to see what we are doing, and to do things at the atomic level, is ultimately developed." And that, in short, is exactly what is happening today. Scientists, from a variety of academic backgrounds, have now developed tools so sensitive that they can "see" and "feel" at the atomic level.

THE TOOLS: OUR EYES, EARS, AND FINGERS

The first microscope was a thousandfold improvement over the human eye. Newer microscopes are a thousandfold more powerful than these microscopes—or a million times more powerful than the human eye. Powerful discoveries are occurring as a result of being able to see at this level. Researchers are learning why the human body lets some cells containing viruses go undetected while eradicating others. This knowledge may help find a cure for a number of viruses, including AIDS.

More sophisticated tools, such the scanning probe microscope (SPM), invented in 1981 by IBM, now provide the means for atoms and molecules to be moved with greater ease and accuracy. In the case of the SPM, voltage delivered through a supersharp tip moves the atoms. The atomic force microscope (AFM), also developed by IBM, probes surfaces and can produce topographical images of individual atoms. The result is that scientists are gaining newfound knowledge about how matter operates and interacts at the atomic and molecular level. This means that they can now begin connecting different molecules—molecules that naturally might never have been put together.

For the first time, biological structures are being observed and modified at the level of the human cell (a red blood cell is 7,000 nanometers in diameter and 2,000 nanometers in height). The implications for human health and the health-care industry are astounding. If researchers can understand how the herpes virus inserts itself into a healthy cell, a solution to the troublesome virus suddenly becomes possible. When this insertion mechanism is understood, scientists may be able to modify the herpes virus with a specific molecular attachment that might render it impotent to invade healthy cells. Think of it as changing the shape of a key so that it can no longer unlock any doors. The chances are that the researchers will be successful. Early last year, the Department of Energy's Pacific Northwest National Laboratory received the world's largest high-performance nuclear magnetic resonance spectrometer, which will allow researchers and scientists to take things to the next level by determining the three-dimensional structure of molecules and view them atom by atom.

The "NanoManipulator," developed by scientists at the University of North Carolina and now produced and marketed by a company called 3rd Tech, located in Raleigh, North Carolina, is allowing researchers not only to see atoms and molecules in 3-D, but also—through the use of a computer—to move, push, prod, and probe atoms and molecules. This capability is leading to increased information about the strength of new materials, how plastics melt, and how DNA works, as well as how the blood cells differ in a hemophiliac and a healthy person.

Physical vapor synthesis (PVS) is another tool helping to advance nanotechnology. PVS is a process that heats materials at temperatures so high that they vaporize. The particles are then cooled at different temperatures and pressures with various gases to create unique nanoparticles. Think of this technique as steam coming off a boiling pot in a kitchen. As the steam collects on a cold window, tiny ice crystals form. Scrape off enough of these crystals, and you can make a new product—a snowball. Granted, a snowball isn't particularly useful, but PVS is allowing companies to produce mass quantities of unique nanocrystals and nanoparticles that are in turn being used in a variety of products today.

And remember, these nanoparticles will be able to do amazing things because at the nanoscale they achieve unique mechanical, optical, strength, conductive, magnetic, and various other characteristics that are not available to their larger bulk-sized material cousins.

Molecular beam epitaxy and organo-metallic vapor epitaxy are yet two other advancements that are allowing the creation of new and vastly higher-functioning products. In spite of their rather ominous-sounding names, the process simply allows for coats of material to be evenly and accurately layered across the surface of another material with atomic precision. Depending on the atomic structure of the material being layered, products will be created that have unique and enhanced thermal, structural, or optical properties. Frictionless bearings, scratch-proof glasses and car paint, better drug delivery, and more powerful fiber-optic cables are just a few of the developments being helped along by these advancements in manufacturing methodology.

Supramolecular chemistry is also making startling advances in understanding how molecules self-assemble. Chemists are now learning how to design molecules to bind to one another in a specific fashion to build a larger system or product. While not typically thought of as a tool in the traditional manufacturing sense, a chemist's beaker must now be thought of as such. The reason is that a tool is any machine or any *process* that can construct something. Therefore, if chemists can now construct something in a beaker, it is fair to consider the chemistry that creates the product a tool. This is just one of the many ways in which nanotechnology will require people to think differently and venture into new arenas in order to survive in this new age.

POWERFUL COMPUTERS AND SOPHISTICATED SOFTWARE

The development of ever-more-powerful computers and more sophisticated software—developments that nanotechnology itself continues to advance—are, in turn, aiding the development of nanotechnology. Just as Boeing can design, test, and "fly" a plane before it is ever built, using advanced modeling programs and computer-aided design (CAD) on powerful computers, nanotechnologists—armed with a better understanding of how atoms and molecules move and operate and vastly more powerful computers—are doing the same to design new materials, new drugs, and more powerful computers. This is a cycle that will only push nanotechnology to ever-greater heights at an ever-quicker pace.

Furthermore, advances in fields like distributed computing, which allows researchers to utilize thousands of idle personal computers and thus match the power of supercomputers, are facilitating solutions to issues as complex as gene sequencing, atmospheric chemistry, and the folding of proteins. Programs that used to take years to sequence the folding of a protein are now taking months. Within a few years, it might be days, hours, minutes, or even seconds if exponential advances in computing continue.

SCALABLE PRODUCTION

In the recent past only a small number of chemists and companies have been able to produce nanoscale materials—and then only in a limited, haphazard, or costly fashion. For example, according to Nanophase Corporation, in the mid-

1990s it cost them $1,000 to produce a single gram of nanoparticles. Today the same product literally costs pennies on the dollar and is being used in everything from odor-eating foot powders and tires to navy ships and automobiles.

Richard Smalley, founder of Carbon Nanotechnologies of Houston, used to produce a very limited number of grams of carbon nanotubes—and then only for highly specialized academic or government research. Today, thanks in part to $15 million in venture capital, the company is on the verge of mass-producing and mass-marketing carbon nanotubes.

In the case of both Nanophase and Carbon Nanotechnologies, the cost of their products continues to decrease while the quantity and quality increases. As the materials become cheaper, engineers and salespersons alike are realizing that engineered solutions to complex or novel problems are now available. For example, whereas before it was too expensive to consider using specialized nanoparticles to replace palladium (another costly material that is used in many automobiles for catalytic conversion), today it is possible—and tomorrow it will be necessary if businesses want to remain competitive.

This scenario will repeat itself almost daily in almost every field. What was once considered impossible or at best impracticable is now possible; and what is possible will soon become inevitable as nanotech attacks thousands of existing products from both a cost and a quality perspective. A 1999 report issued by the World Technology Evaluation Center concluded that we are now only seeing "the tip of the iceberg or the pinnacle of the pyramid" with regard to these new materials.

CROSS FERTILIZATION OF IDEAS

Unlike most academic disciplines, nanotechnology does not neatly fit into one specific discipline. In fact, it is at the center of many areas of science including chemistry, engineering, biology, materials science, physics, and information sciences. Because of the cross-disciplinary nature of the research, scientists who might never have interacted are now working closely together. The result is an explosion of new developments. As Chad Mirkin, Director of Northwestern University's Institute of Nanotechnology, said, "At the nanolevel, atoms do not belong to any one field of science." This means that material scientists, as they attempt to develop the next generation of materials for the space shuttle, are now talking to biologists to understand how natural systems manipulate atoms.

A case in point: Biologists are helping material scientists understand how the simple abalone can take calcium carbonate—the same material that makes up common (and crumbly) schoolroom chalk—and make a seashell that is three thousand times stronger than chalk. Similarly, medical professionals who are attempting to solve complex health problems at the molecular level are now speaking with mechanical engineers to help them develop tools that mimic the motors in ATP—an enzyme in the human body. To mechanical engineers' amazement, ATP, a chemical, fuels a shaft and a rotor that operate just like a motor but are a thousand times smaller than anything man has built. This suggests that even Mother Nature has something to teach today's brightest engineers in terms of miniaturization and self-assembly.

In many ways, nanotechnology scientists are like very young children who have just comprehended what Legos are while simultaneously gaining the manual dexterity to put those blocks together. And like an infant, these scientists are growing up very fast. If you are to keep up, you must begin changing and learning today.

NANOPOINTS

* How would your products change if you could manipulate the properties of their raw materials?
* How prepared for radical change are you? Who in your company is responsible for tracking technological developments?
* How might vastly more powerful computers help your company redesign your product, create entirely new products, or assist you in designing a more efficient inventory or distribution network?

CHAPTER TWO

Interesting – But What Do I Have to Do?

"BECAUSE THE NANOWORLD IS DIFFERENT FROM
THE MACROWORLD, MORE IMAGINATION AND
CREATIVE THINKING ARE NEEDED."

—MIKE ROCO

As we have shown, nanotechnology will dramatically change the technology fabric of the world. The ability to design and define the world at the atomic level will blur the lines that separate the classical sciences, create entire new educational disciplines, and essentially change the way we view medicine, prevention, and treatment.

It will also impact what has become standard operating procedure for the business world. Certainly, non-nano companies will continue to flourish. However, few companies will be left totally untouched, and the effects are many. Companies will develop stronger relationships with universities, becoming more active in areas of basic research and relying on these relationships to provide highly educated future employees. Employee incentive programs will change from one-time awards to long-term programs that acknowledge the initial idea, the product prototype, and the final production. Longer term incentive programs will also enhance employee retention. Corporate financial metrics will no longer focus only on short-term opportunities; businesses will develop long-range (fifteen-year) investment strategies—perhaps differentiating short-term and long-term companies to stockholders. Corporations will become a melting pot not of racial diversity but of technical diversity, bringing together all aspects of the sciences. In short, nanotechnology will radically change how you, the executive, plan and run your business.

Because nanotech is still in its infancy, however, there aren't any paradigms for how best to incorporate it into business. Many corporations are at a loss as to how to proceed. They don't have the right people, they're not sure how much to invest, and they're not sure when to make a move. For example, Lockheed Martin and Boeing (giants in the aerospace and space industry) acknowledge that nanotech will have a significant impact on their products. Although both companies are involved in and aware of nanotechnology, the implementation into their products will be "slow and careful." Both have the dual goals of not missing the boat and not heading in the wrong direction, so they are cautiously analyzing and monitoring the technology, asking the right questions and looking for the best solution. This chapter provides a framework for asking the right questions and finding a solution for you.

As an executive . . .

- You will need to modify your thinking, your methodologies, and your measurement tools.

- You must be willing to expand your definition of core competencies and the requirements for your technical staff.
- You must be willing to look at industries and products far removed from your own for the breakthrough innovations that can revolutionize your company.
- You must be willing to allocate a portion of your budget for ideas or training that may not show short-term results but could dominate the longer forecast.
- You must be able to accommodate in your strategic processes longer-term goals and different measurement metrics.
- You will work not only with your customers to determine their changing needs, but you will also work with your colleagues to create new products, markets, and customers.

Preparing your company for the implementation and integration of nanotechnology into your products and services will require a comprehensive assessment and plan. There are six major areas to look at.

1. Employee motivation and reward systems
2. Talent recruitment and consulting support
3. Corporate and competitor strengths
4. Research and development investment
5. Strategic planning and financial management
6. Standard processes and methodologies

These six factors are interdependent and may overlap in many companies. All of them, however, will have to change if your company wants to stay ahead of the competition.

EMPLOYEE MOTIVATION AND REWARD SYSTEMS

The breadth of nanotech and its potential to impact multiple segments and aspects of any business will require rethinking the incentive process. First, employees will need to be rewarded for cross-disciplinary actions and inventions. Incentive programs today dole out rewards based on the overall success of the entire company and often provide additional incentives associated with individual business unit success. The truth is, joint programs are often hindered by the latter type of reward, which can generate a stovepipe mentality and trigger many internal battles over maintaining single business segment goals. The interdisciplinary nature of nanotechnology will require that diverse groups within the corporation work together, sharing technology, information, contacts, funding, and resources to maximize the value and growth. It is critical that some portion of the Three Musketeers mentality be infused into the corporate culture and incentive plans. In fact, one approach is to reward the employee who *does* see across division boundaries and works to bring units together to create the greatest benefit for the corporation. This is just not happening yet in today's corporations.

Second, nanotechnology infusion will not be a one-shot deal, and therefore incentive plans and reward systems may also take a different approach to timing. Because nanotechnology is in its infancy, some ideas or strategies may not bear fruit for five to ten years. Also, the time to enter a new market or create a new "societal need" may be longer than the standard calendar year. In these cases, employees may receive some innovation award when the idea is conceived or patented and receive additional awards for bringing the idea to market at a much later date.

3M, with its high level of product and technology diversity, long-term vision, and over 17 separate employee reward programs, has systems similar to the latter recommended above. One award acknowledges innovation or an idea while another program, the Golden Step Award, recognizes the development of new products from that innovation.

Your sales force and their incentive plans may also need modification as nanotech is introduced into your corporation. In the future your sales people may not just sell pre-existing products out of a catalog, they may instead tailor each product for individual customers. They will need to become more technically savvy, and they will need to listen carefully to customer needs and priorities to foster long-term partnerships and teaming. The incentive plans should not only cover rewards for amount of products sold, but also rewards for intangibles such as exploring new markets, increasing customer satisfaction, establishing partnerships and teaming arrangements, or recognizing a new customer or societal need. All of these will be a part of exploiting nanotechnology advances and research. Granted, it is much easier to reward countable items, such as number of products sold, but to take advantage of the innovation and creativity in a sales force armed with nanotech product potential, corporations will need to figure out how to measure and reward ideas and partnerships.

TALENT RECRUITMENT AND CONSULTING SUPPORT

At this time, there is not a single corporation or government entity that has the inclusive knowledge to fully take advantage of the potential of nanotechnology. Universities, with their multiple colleges, perhaps come closest to the technically integrated ideal. Your organization, for example, probably has a well-defined set of knowledge requirements for the technical talent recruited into the organization. If you produce computer hardware, you look for systems engineers, software experts, electrical engineers, and electronic-manufacturing experts. If your product is in the medical field, you look for biologists, device mechanical engineers, and people with the knowledge to manufacture biological-related systems. With the introduction of nanotechnology into the entire market segment, these guidelines become very blurred. Computer manufacturers, for example, may need biologists to implement a molecular computer approach (as opposed to traditional silicon-based electronics). Medical-device companies might need computer-simulation experts to predict and model the biological interactions at the atomic scale. With the ability of nanotechnology to merge biological and electronic systems, health-care providers may find that they need significant electrical-engineering expertise in addition to their biology knowledge strength.

This multidisciplined disruptive nature of nanotechnology will require the merging of many scientific disciplines that, so far, have remained fairly distinct. This will generate entirely new areas of expertise. Just as the discipline of computer engineering evolved from the combination of electrical engineering, software, and other disciplines, the nano-engineer will evolve from the combination of many fields. For example, a degree in nanobioengineering may include training in molecular biology, electrical engineering, and computer architecture and result in a career in molecular computing. A nano-materials engineer may study mechanical engineering, quantum physics, and manufacturing methods and work in the field of nanomaterials development for an aircraft manufacturer.

This required merging of technical disciplines and per-sonnel is not a trivial task. Each discipline has its own vocabulary and approach to development and problem-solving. It will require an enlightened leader to merge dis-ciplines and personnel into a strong synergy as well as to use this combined talent effectively to the benefit of the product or company. Possible methods include provid-ing internal seminars—with executive attendance—where various technical disciplines and activities are discussed, or retaining guest speakers from outside of your industry at employee meetings. The executive could support interde-partmental discussions and convey an openness to new technical areas and expertise. A culture of encouragement to pursue different ideas must be nurtured in order to pro-vide the best assessment for a given technology oppor-tunity. Yet it is often difficult for a dyed-in-the-wool, electrical-engineering-trained executive to see *any* correla-tion to, say, biology. Too often it is easier to scoff at the unknown than to try to understand its relevance. An en-lightened executive, however, will be the first to ask in-sightful questions and show interest in a new idea or field, and he or she will reap the benefits of nanotechnology.

Many companies are creating strong relationships with research institutions to address the issues of tech-nology development and multiple technical disciplines. For example, in Minnesota there are at least six corpora-tions in partnership at some level with each nanotech-nology initiative at the University of Minnesota. We'll discuss more about the research aspect a little later, but the secondary advantage to this type of partnership is that companies have the opportunity to hire graduate students or others who have worked with their particular technology while in school. This collaboration provides a ready pool of qualified and knowledgeable potential employees as well as employees that are well connected with state-of-the-art research.

Forward-thinking companies will also want to prepare their future employees. Because of the technical breadth and multidiscipline aspect of nanotechnology, educational institutions will need to modify and enhance their academic programs. Industry can provide valuable assistance, guidance, and insight to our educational structure by working closely with these institutions to develop the curriculum and guidance for what is needed in future technical employees. One thing your company can do now is to let the educational institutions in your area know that you are interested by calling college deans and finding out how you can support curriculum development. Another idea is to talk to your employees who have recently graduated to get their input on how curricula may improve their preparation for a career.

The use of consultants will also change. In most cases today, the technical consultant hired has knowledge in a field or area closely related to the core competencies of the company. Rarely does a computer company hire a molecular biologist to help in product development. With the advent of nanotechnology, however, this will no longer be the case. In fact, as an enlightened executive, you may decide that the first step toward understanding nanotechnology and its impact on your product and marketplace is to hire consultants in unrelated fields to come in and shake up the corporate scientific culture before actually hiring a biologist to interact with your software engineers.

CORPORATE AND COMPETITOR STRENGTHS

It is human nature to view your strengths in a positive light and those of your competitors with a jaundiced eye. If, however, there is a time to be keenly aware of what your competitors are doing, it is now. You need to pay attention to their investments and partnerships. What type of resources are they hiring, and what areas are they moving in? Often employees will publish technical papers discussing new advances—not necessarily product-related. These technical papers can provide insight into the technical direction of the competition and where they may be headed. There is a great deal of publicly available information that will provide valuable insights into what may be on the horizon. The bottom line is, don't assume that your competition is merrily following the same path. There are many examples in which non-U.S. companies have taken over traditional U.S. markets (cars, TVs, radios, etc.) with better technology at a lower price. Perhaps, if those U.S. companies had been watching what their foreign competitors were up to from a technical standpoint, they would not have been blindsided by their advances. Just because your competition has always been Company B in the vitamin business does not mean that it isn't planning to steal your previously untouched therapeutic wound-dressing business. With nanotechnology, it may be easier for companies to expand into new and seemingly unrelated markets that compete with yours.

You also need to view your own corporate strengths in a different light and with broader vision. You need to see how you can leverage your core competencies and abilities into not only new segments of your known market, but into totally new markets. How can you apply what you already know, enhanced by nanotech initiatives, to move into a new market or, better yet, create one where no market existed? For example, if your company provides automated spraying systems for paint application to commercial buildings, how can your system be modified to apply "paint" containing bacteria-killing biological materials to the walls of operating rooms? Will you need to modify pressure, applied paint thickness, or paint containers? Will you need to control the temperature of the applied substance? If your automated spraying system can be made portable, perhaps it has application in the civil emergency sector or for military units operating in isolated areas, or perhaps your approach could provide a decontamination methodology not currently employed.

Looking at the larger picture and being willing to consider seemingly unrelated opportunities is easier said than done. The changes required can be brought about by actions such as the following:

1. Looking outside your corporate market segment for new information
2. Bringing in experts outside of your traditional technology discipline
3. Looking for emerging trends
4. Paying attention to your scientists and engineers for evolving technology

RESEARCH AND DEVELOPMENT INVESTMENT

Traditionally, most of the funds expended for R&D are focused on the "development" aspect of the process and on products applicable to the present market segment. There are certainly notable exceptions to this statement, where a significant amount of money is spent on research, but even then much of the research is based on the core competencies of the company. Very rarely would a company such as, say, Hostess, spend R&D dollars on a tangential industry like vitamin supplements or a market like aromatherapy. Yet this may indeed be the case with nanotechnology, in which traditional food items can be enhanced by nutritional supplements and even scents that increase taste sensation. People may not only purchase Twinkies for their creamy filling, but also for the full RDA of twenty-five different vitamins/minerals, and, voilà!, Hostess is competing with One a Day.

By looking outside your company's traditional industry, you can better prepare for the potential impact of nanotechnology on your current product or capability. This doesn't mean that your business or every company needs to set up a state-of-the-art nanotechnology lab. After all, the initial research is usually carried out in a handful of industry, academic, and government facilities and not in hundreds of labs. Most likely, this will remain the case for much of nanotechnology development. What will change, from a business perspective, is the need for corporate America to be aware of and, at some level, participate in this basic research. The involvement may come about by attending nearby university symposiums or having a member of your staff serve as a liaison with universities. In fact, this is happening at many universities and in almost every state. Industry is becoming more and more involved with basic research programs. Industry involvement includes the giants (3M, Cargill, IBM, Hewlett-Packard, Merck, Boeing, etc.), as well as many of the small start-up companies mentioned throughout this book. Companies large and small are partnering with research organizations not only to have access to the developed technology, but also to take advantage of the access to all disciplines that is possible with a university partner.

According to *MIT Technology Review,* Agilent Technologies and Harvard University are working on materials with nano-sized pores that can analyze DNA, and engeneOS/MIT and Nanosphere/Northwestern University both have teams working with gold nanoparticles; the first studying remote control of biological molecules and the latter working on detectors to sense DNA and pathogens. Ways of sensing biological molecules are also being studied by a team from Molecular Nanosystems and Stanford University, which is working with carbon nanotubes, and a Nanosys/Harvard University team, which is using nanowires.

This recommended early involvement is driven by the rapid pace of development in nanotechnology. Because this field covers so many disciplines, it is to the benefit of industry to be involved in the embryonic research stages. Participation may include graduate-student fellowships, joint research with your company, or even a laboratory commitment. Creating this early involvement allows industry to take advantage of and in some cases direct the path for specific basic research-development efforts.

Motorola, which is focusing on the physics of the interaction of molecules and their specific properties, is a good example of this type of research partnership stepped up to the international level. Although Motorola has worked closely with Rice University in the United States, it also has personnel at research labs in France and Japan, with each group investigating different aspects of fundamental physics. When discussing the Motorola approach to intellectual property protection at the international level, Dr. Herb Goronkin, vice president and director of Motorola's Physical Research Labs, stated, "Our approach is simple—what we invent together, we share."

Beyond the participation in the basic research stages of nanotechnology, there are varying degrees of additional involvement. In many cases, as nanotechnology initially seeps into the business world, the investment may be as small as a few journal subscriptions or allowing your technical staff some hours to explore a specific scientific area. You may consider online access to multidisciplinary information-based services provided by federal or private sectors. As the technology progresses, investment may increase to participation in multiple conferences or development committees or instituting an internal program to train multiple engineers in nanotechnology. The other end of this investment spectrum is the option for significant investment, such as funding and developing technologies and capabilities internally or with partnered research institutions or companies. Other examples of this type of significant investment are the extensive research labs owned by IBM, Hewlett-Packard, and 3M. The question is, how do you decide at what level to invest?

Three Factors to Consider When Deciding on an Investment Strategy for Nanotechnology

Determining investment levels is not simply a matter of how many R&D dollars are in the budget or which areas may be deemed most interesting. There are many factors that can have a significant influence on the final investment decision. Relying on only one of these factors or some other consideration will result in a less-than-optimal approach. The three factors discussed here are as follows:

1. Technology maturity
2. Potential revenue impact
3. Competitors' investment

Technology Maturity

The maturity of the technology will drive not only the initial investment decision but also the timing of increased financial commitment. Fueled by investment, interest, and industry application, all technology will naturally move through stages—from the initial idea, to understanding and potential application, then on to application refinement and production.

For a technology that is currently at an early stage of maturity, investment at the lowest levels is probably appropriate in most cases. For example, if your company has a potential application for an implantable, automatic drug-delivery system, you may choose to watch developments at universities as well as monitor government policy regarding implantable nanotechnology. These activities are at the lower level of investment/commitment and also appropriate since the technical maturity of the implantable nanodevices is low; it is still barely more than a neat idea that is somewhat understood. Based on the forecasted maturity of that technology, investment may increase as time progresses. Since technology can change more quickly or slowly than predicted, proposed investment strategies that cover multiple years should include a degree of flexibility.

An example of the relationship between technology maturity and investment level over time is shown in Figure 2.1. Note that the technology maturity phases overlap in the upper portion of the chart, which represents the uncertainty in the speed of technology evolution. These overlapping regions can be taken into account in the investment strategy, as shown by the solid, dotted, and dashed lines at the bottom of the chart, where each line represents a different investment strategy.

Returning to our example of the implantable, automated drug-delivery system, the top line shows an aggressive and significant investment strategy representative of a company that knows clearly that this technology is applicable to them and is willing to invest significantly at the beginning to get a piece of the technology (perhaps via a patent or two). The middle line of the chart shows a company that is monitoring the technical maturity very closely.

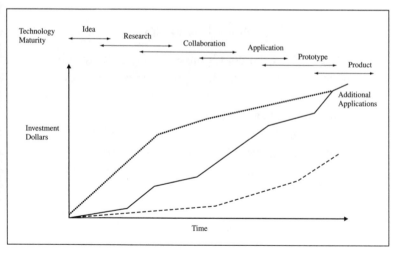

Figure 2.1 Various investment scenarios.

Initially investment is low because the company may be skeptical of the technology feasibility or its application. As the technology matures, the decision is made to invest in a step-by-step fashion, but still at a moderate investment amount. This middle-line company will leverage off of the developments of a company heavily investing—like the top-line company. Finally, the lower line represents a minimal investment during multiple phases of technology maturity. This type of investment is representative of a company that may be tangentially interested in the technology. In our example, it does not represent a company that plans to sell imbedded devices or chemicals, but rather one that may be interested in diseases in plants that could benefit from automatic delivery systems. The technology is of interest, but because only a portion, say 25 percent, is directly applicable to the company, its executives need to be aware of what is happening but don't need to be a major player or owner of the technology.

Potential Revenue Impact

Although the technology's stage of maturity may point to one level of investment, analysis of the potential revenue impact may negate the decision or, conversely, may drive the investment to a higher level. It's like making ice cubes. Even though the "technology" is very mature, companies in arctic regions probably don't care about the capability, whereas folks in equatorial regions may choose to invest a great deal in creating cheaper ice cubes.

A technology that could potentially increase revenue, profitability, market share, or any financial return criteria by tenfold or greater should warrant increased investment. The increased investment could be used to have multiple engineers become knowledgeable in the technology, thereby allowing a broader understanding base within the company, i.e., more money spent at the awareness level. This use of investment dollars overlaps with the requirement to have a technically diverse and knowledgeable workforce. Additional investment could also provide participation at higher levels, for example, by having company representatives become more involved with the research centers. Or perhaps the additional investment could be used to accelerate progression of the technology. In this last situation, investment may be in the form of a research grant to the educational institution performing the work.

Competitors' Investment

Even if the technology is at a very early maturity level, if your competition is supporting the technology, it may be worthwhile to take a look at greater participation and investment from your company. Of course, the motivation for your competitors' investment should be evaluated since there are many reasons for a high investment level. For instance, your company may compete with 3M in the tape market. You observe that 3M is investing significantly in biological nanoparticles. Now, this does not mean your company needs to pursue biological nanoparticles, because 3M is also a significant player in the pharmaceutical arena and it makes sense for them to investigate that technology. So even though 3M is your competitor, it is not necessary for your tape company to seek biological nanoparticle patents. The important aspect of this assessment is that if a technology is forecasted to have a large impact in your market, you want to ensure access to that technology and not let your competitors get the upper hand through sole-teaming agreements with research organizations, patents, trademarks, and so on. Many large companies are making significant investments, and many of these will be discussed in the next chapter.

STRATEGIC PLANNING

Nanotechnology will also impact the process you use to assess and forecast your business future. In addition to requiring a revision of how R&D dollars are allocated, nanotechnology will require a longer-term view of funds invested in "research." In general, many executives would prefer to invest in technologies or projects that will provide near-term (two- to five-year) results. This will *not* be the case with nanotechnology. Many of the developments and technologies discussed in this book will not truly be strong revenue producers for another ten years or more. This stands the current approach of near-term returns on research-and-development dollars on its head. Executives need to have a longer-term focus and be patient for returns. Of course, the choice can always be made to invest minimally or not at all and wait for the technology or market to appear. As mentioned above, because of the rapid change and critical breakthroughs that happen daily in the nanotechnology field, this is a dangerous position. A strong market leader can easily be blindsided and overrun by a smaller company that was aware of the innovations and leveraged that awareness.

An example of a company that will not be blindsided easily is Hewlett-Packard. HP has always been very successful at inventing, developing, and implementing new-product technology in the expected three- to five-year time frame. However, in 1995, David Packard realized that some new technologies that would have significant impact on HP business, in particular nanotechnology, would also require longer to develop. So in that year HP established the Quantum Science Research Department, which has the charter to do basic research in areas that have plausible application to HP products. The name of the department represents the intent to focus on nanotechnology, since quantum sciences deal with the physics of the forces and interactions that occur distinctly at the atomic level. HP hired known leaders in physics, chemistry, and other scientific fields to lead the organization. The combination of people from multiple technical disciplines coupled with the long-term charter and funding commitment is what has helped to place HP as a leader today in the nanotechnology field. Other companies such as AT&T and IBM also have this far-reaching vision and commitment. These companies are not only examples of long-term strategic thinking, but exemplify investment in basic research, partnerships with universities, and striving for technical diversity in their workforce.

One of the most important impacts on strategic planning is that the metrics used to assess the validity of a new market, product, or research investment must be modified to address the long-range potential of nanotechnology. In many cases today, investment dollars spent on a product (development or improvement) are expected to break even in three years or so, and this is how the progress or success of a development investment is measured.

Nanotechnology, because of its infancy, will take longer, in most cases, to reach that point—perhaps eight to twelve years. Therefore, it is not appropriate to expect nanotech development to use the three-year breakeven criterion as a benchmark of success. Instead, measurement criteria should include technical milestones, breakthroughs, partnering agreements, and competitor actions. The success of the development and investment can be measured by the progress through these milestones over a longer period—and not just by the revenue produced. The executive must be conscientiously aware that long-term nanotech-related development, investigations, or partnerships may appear unsuccessful without using these modified metrics.

One solution to the dilemma of long-term investments and short-term revenue goals is to spin off the development aspect of the business. This cleanly separates the sets of goals and measurement criteria and reduces tension on both sides. In fact, today many nanotechnology ideas or technologies are spun off as separate companies because it is easier to allow the traditional company to respond to Wall Street and allow the development, start-up company to do the research and development, especially in long-term areas such as nanotechnology. NanoTex from Burlington Fabrics, Carbon Nanotubes from Rice University, and AVEKA from 3M are good spinoff examples. In this situation, they have access to venture capital and also often are getting some funding and a promise of potential business from their parent company or organization.

Whatever solution may be chosen, with its development-and-research investments, nanotechnology will require modification to the traditional strategic-planning process.

STANDARD PROCESSES AND METHODOLOGIES

As nanotechnology is folded into your products, modification will be required in areas such as manufacturing processes and quality control. As you are considering both the benefits of and investment required for nanotechnology, it is necessary to remember that dealing with nanometers will require changes in basic processes. Going back to the example of bacteria-killing paint, the process of applying the paint may not be changed at all. However, requirements for mixing the paint with the additives and maintaining paint temperature during transportation and application will require new manuals and training for employees. Also, because the new antibacterial paint may need to be cleaned in a special way to ensure its effectiveness, labels and instructions will have to be changed. This is a fairly simple example, but in other cases entire pieces of equipment will need to be replaced or modified. With each change, documentation and training will require modification. Processes that have been perfected with years of constant improvement will no longer be valid.

Quality control will be impacted because with nanotechnology both "quality" and "control" may take on new ramifications. Measuring in individual atoms and molecules creates a much stricter definition of both. The multidiscipline aspect of nanotechnology may require that your QA engineers be skilled not only in semiconductors or paint-color consistency, but also in molecular computers or biological bacteria and measuring their concentration effectively. It is the change between measuring macro quantities or properties to measuring and understanding quality at the atomic level. Hence the impact of nanotechnology on manufacturing processes and QA will be much more that just another revision of the manual; it will be a revolutionary change in how manufacturing and product verification is viewed and exercised.

Several companies are already anticipating this need. NPoint, in Wisconsin, has developed a line of innovative devices that can move nanoparticles around. These devices and systems will quickly evolve to having the capability to control and measure attributes at the atomic level—a critical aspect of nanotech quality control. Other companies, such as Queensgate in England and Physik Instrument of Germany, also are poised to address the issue of manufacturing and measurement at the nanometer scale.

Your quality-control and manufacturing processes may not be impacted during the early stages of nanotechnology integration, but as the technology matures and is introduced into your product lines, these segments will have a critical influence. As they say, forewarned is forearmed.

NANOPOINTS

* How can you reward your employees for ideas, innovation, and cross-functional activities?
* Are you looking outside of your industry for new talent and potential expansion?
* Are you an enlightened leader—encouraging new ideas, innovation, and multi-disciplined employees and groups?
* Do you know what your competitors are up to?
* Are there nearby universities that can support technology

development for your company? Are you familiar with their strengths? Do they know your needs?

* Is your research and development plan consistent with the maturity of the technology?
* Do your strategic planning processes and financial measurement tools allow for long-term development and a degree of flexibility?
* Are you planning for changes in manufacturing methods and quality control programs?

CHAPTER THREE

Follow the Money, Follow the Leaders

"SOMEONE NEEDS TO GO OUT, PUT A FLAG IN THE GROUND AND SAY: 'NANOTECHNOLOGY: THIS IS WHERE WE ARE GOING TO GO.'"

—DR. RICHARD SMALLEY, IN TESTIMONY BEFORE CONGRESS, JUNE 22, 1999.

THE GOVERNMENT

The Internet, radar, Velcro, Tang, and even the bar codes that help speed you through the checkout line at the grocery store are just a few of the advances brought to us courtesy of the federal government, believe it or not.

Most of the research in the aforementioned technologies and products did not start out with the goal of revolutionizing society, transforming an industry, or helping the average citizen get through the grocery store quicker. Rather, they were technologies and applications that spun off from one use (often military), and some ingenious person recognized that there were additional—and profitable—uses of the technology.

Developments in nanotechnology will likely occur in much the same manner. The difference with nanotechnology, however, is that government researchers and scientists are confident that nanotechnology *is* going to revolutionize entire industries and society. Charles Campbell, codirector of the University of Washington's Center for Nanotechnology, summed up this sentiment perfectly: "It is widely recognized throughout the research community, both in academia and industry, that the next century will be dominated by developments in nanotechnology just as the past quarter of a century has been dominated by microtechnology." And according to a report issued in 2000 by the National Science and Technology Council, "The total societal impact of nanotechnology is expected to be much greater than silicon . . . because it is applicable in many more fields than electronics." The problem is that it isn't entirely clear just *how* society will be transformed.

It was precisely this anticipation of the unknown, spurred on by inspirational testimony from leading scientists and industry leaders in the late 1990s, that led President Clinton to fund the National Nanotechnology Initiative at a level of $422 million in his last year in office. The strategic importance of the technology prompted the Bush Administration to increase funding by more than 50 percent, to $710 million, for 2003. And funding will likely increase further due to the tragic events of September 11, 2001 (nanotechnology has a wide variety of applications for homeland security), and because President Bush's science adviser, John Marburger, the former director of the Brookhaven National Laboratory, is well grounded in nanotechnology and understands its importance.

The United States is not alone in its efforts to develop nanotechnology. The government of Japan, at the request of their powerful business lobby, Keiranden, which sees nanotechnology as a national priority, is investing $465 million a year. Other countries investing in nanotechnology are South Korea ($200 million), China (an estimated $200 million), Canada ($120 million), Taiwan ($110 million), Israel ($100 million), and Australia ($50 million). Russia, Germany, Britain, France, and a host of other smaller countries are also making similar investments in nanotechnology. In total, worldwide investment in the field is approximately $2 billion, suggesting that while the U.S. might be the largest investor, its leadership is by no means secure.

The stakes are high. Nanotechnology's importance to advanced materials, electronics, and chemical and biological detection and treatment is driving the military establishment to invest seriously in nanotechnology. Its many space-related applications—in the form of creating smaller, lighter, and longer-lasting materials—are fueling NASA's interest, and its relevance to the early detection and treatment of a variety of diseases—through improved therapeutics, diagnostics, and biomaterials—is prompting the National Institutes of Health's interest. The Department of Transportation is interested in "smart" (e.g., self-cleaning or self-repairing), lightweight, affordable materials, while the Department of Energy is focused on the implications for energy and the environment. And working with all of these agencies is the National Institute of Standards and Technology, which is facilitating the development of new equipment and new standards.

The line between national security, material science, transportation, health-care, and environmental applications becomes easily blurred with commercial applications. For example, the U.S. Army is investing heavily in nanotechnology in the hope that it will help create materials that can make uniforms that will simultaneously monitor a soldier's health, detect and detoxify chemical agents, heat and cool the soldier as appropriate, and independently generate power so the soldier's "wearable" computer can wirelessly remain in constant communication with headquarters. Any one of these applications, if successful, will have wide-ranging ramifications on the clothing, health-care, or telecommunications industries.

And it is these economic applications that are driving a number of individual states to jump-start public–private nanotechnology projects at the state level. In 2001, California and New York both kicked off multihundred-million-dollar nanotechnology initiatives. In the case of California, the state is contributing $100 million, and Hewlett-Packard, Sun Microsystems, and Sequenom are adding millions more to establish the California Nano-Systems Institute. They hope it will provide California corporations with cutting-edge research and in the process help maintain the state's leadership position in a variety of fields. New York's $50 million program, matched by a $100 million contribution from IBM, is similar in nature, with the goal being to establish the state as a leader in the promising new field of nanoelectronics.

Texas, New Mexico, Pennsylvania, Indiana, Florida, and Illinois are also engaged in similar, albeit smaller-scale, efforts. The logic behind the investments is simple: economic development. A small investment might reap a huge return. According to Michael Cox, a Federal Reserve Bank senior vice-president, the fortunes of nanotechnology "could dwarf Bill Gates."

The central building block in most state efforts is a strong and reputable program at either a university or a federal laboratory. In the case of California, activity is centered at two University of California campuses, Los Angeles and Santa Barbara. In New York, the State University of New York at Albany is heavily involved in nanotechnology, along with Cornell, Columbia, and Rensselaer and the federal government's Brookhaven National Laboratory. In Texas, Rice University and the University of Texas (both Dallas and Austin) play leading roles together with NASA's Johnson Space Center in Houston. In Illinois, Northwestern University and Argonne National Laboratory are the drivers, and the federal laboratories at Sandia and Los Alamos are integral to New Mexico's efforts.

In September 2001, the federal government designated six Centers of Excellence in nanotechnology. See Figure 3.1 for a list and their focus areas. Each center received approximately $12 million, which it will use to perform research within the focus area and attract nanotechnology's brightest academic stars. In turn, these stars will attract the best graduate students, making these centers excellent sources for future recruitment.

The six Centers of Excellence were not the only places to receive funding in 2002. Duke, Northwestern, Purdue, and the University of Washington all established nanotechnology centers, joining the University of Michigan, Georgia Tech, Harvard, and Stanford. The prospect that a nanotechnology center is located near you is growing more likely almost every day. With more than one hundred U.S. universities involved in nanotechnology, it is not too soon for companies in search of promising technologies or licensing opportunities to establish formal

UNIVERSITY	TOPIC	FOCUS AREAS
Columbia University	Center for Electronic Transport in Molecular Nanostructures	Collaboration with industry partners. Potential applications in electronics, biology, neuroscience, etc.
Cornell University	Center for Nanoscale Systems in Information Technologies	Information storage, high-performance electronics, communication and sensor technologies.
Harvard University	Center for the Science of Nanoscale Systems	Exploring properties of nanostructures for novel electric and magnetic devices and quantum information processing.
Northwestern University	Center for Integrated Nanopatterning and Detection Technologies	Nanopatterning in soft materials with potential application to chemical and biological sensors.
Rensselaer Polytechnic Institute	Center for Directed Assembly of Nanostructures	Assembly of nanoscale building blocks to design materials with applications as composites in drug delivery and sensors.
Rice University	Center for Biological and Environmental Nanotechnology	Bioengineering and environmental engineering, integrating biology with nanochemistry.

Figure 3.1 Nanotechnology Centers of Excellence and focus areas.

relations with the technology-transfer offices of these institutions.

Progress, however, is not limited to U.S. universities. In Japan alone, the University of Tokyo, Osaka University, and the Tokyo Institute of Technology have opened nanotechnology research institutions. China has begun operating facilities in Shanghai, and in Israel, Ben Gurion University opened a $100 million center and Hebrew University has established a $40 million center. Such investments warrant close monitoring because technology development is occurring so fast that countries have the potential to leapfrog almost overnight.

For example, Israeli researchers claim the ability to produce industrial-sized batches of pure metal nanopowders at a rate of one hundred kilograms a day—a rate far exceeding the few grams that U.S. institutions are reporting. If true, these nanopowders could be integrated with polymers to construct plastics that are stronger, lighter, and more heat- and radiation-resistant than today's best materials—at a much lower cost. The implications for space-related applications alone are huge.

A second but often overlooked role of government is that of purchaser. Up until 1964, the U.S. government was the sole purchaser of integrated circuits. By accounting for 100 percent of the market, the government provided vital financial support to this strategically important sector. And the scale of the government's purchasing was instrumental in driving production costs down to the point that the technology became affordable to the private sector. Ultimately, the price decreased to the point that computers, operated by powerful integrated circuits, are now a common household amenity.

A closer look at the emerging field of carbon nanotubes, which are examined in greater detail in the next chapter, might illustrate a similar case. Presently the cost of a gram of single-walled carbon tubes is in the neighborhood of $500. This price limits its use to those areas where performance is at a premium. Many of these "premium performance" uses are the current purview of government. For example, it costs NASA $10,000 to launch a pound of material into space and another $20,000 to $50,000 to maintain that material once it is in space. If carbon nanotubes can significantly decrease the weight of numerous materials and ensure they last longer once they get in space, $500 a gram might seem like a bargain. By providing makers of carbon nanotubes a market for their product, the government is helping to bring the cost of these precious materials down. What is today limited to high-cost space applications may be in your car, bike, or golf club tomorrow.

BIG BUSINESS

Hewlett-Packard has publicly said that the majority of its long-range R&D budget is dedicated to nanotechnology. Beyond that, it is hard to get many companies, whether publicly or privately owned, to talk about their forays into this field. This does not mean, however, that it is not happening. Often, what we see reflects only a small portion of the complete picture. Here are some of the things that we do know. (Ironically Japan, which is known for its closed nature, has been very open about its plans for nanotechnology.)

- **Hitachi,** a global leader in the electronics industry, has reorganized itself into cross-disciplinary teams to better take advantage of opportunities in nanotechnology. The goal it has laid out for itself is to become the global leader in electronics. To this end, it is now developing single-electron devices for memory and logic, which would represent revolutionary change in both the amount of data that could be stored, the speed with which it could be retrieved, and the overall computational power of computers.

- Another Japanese company, **Fujitsu,** is building a nano-technology research center to facilitate the production of an ultrafast computer.
- **Toray Industries,** another Japanese company, has spent $40 million to build a center to encourage experts in fields of both nanotechnology and biotechnology to work in closer collaboration in the search for new materials.
- **Mitsubishi** has established a new company for the mass production of carbon fullerene molecules. Its goal is to increase annual production from just under one-half ton today to 3,000 tons a year by 2007—a 6,000-fold increase. By doing so, Mitsubishi hopes to have its products being used in everything from anticancer drugs to longer-lasting batteries and skin-care products. (Fullerenes are a class of cagelike compounds made of carbon rings. The category encompasses both carbon nanotubes and bucky-balls, which are round fullerenes ranging in size from twenty to over five hundred carbon atoms. The most famous is the buckminsterfullerene, which has exactly sixty carbon atoms and looks like a soccer ball but is so named because it also resembles the geodesic dome shapes made famous by Buckminster Fuller.)
- **Mitsui,** on the other hand, spent $15 million to open a facility in 2002 capable of producing 150 tons of carbon nanotubes per year. It plans on marketing its product to automakers, resin makers, and battery makers. (The latter is a market that Nippon Electric Corporation and Sony have already moved into, unveiling a carbon-based battery—a product they claim will lead to laptop computers and cell phones that won't have to be charged for weeks on end.)
- **Asahi Glass Company** is working with nanoparticles and nanocrystals in an effort to create high-performance glass

(e.g., self-cleaning, streak-resistant, light-adjusting)—a worldwide market worth billions.

- **Procter & Gamble** and **British Aerospace** have formed a partnership to create multidisciplinary centers of excellence for nanotechnology.

In the United States, in addition to Hewlett-Packard, IBM and Lucent have occasionally announced some of their more promising nanotechnology developments, specifically in using carbon nanotubes in the next generation of computers. Their rationale for investing is best summed up by Dr. Herb Goronkin of Motorola—another company investing in nanotechnology—who said, "We want to position ourselves either to be one of the discoverers of the replacement for the transistor or, second best, to be able to operate in the world that's created if someone else invents it first."

Eli Lilly, Merck, GlaxoSmithKline, Abbott Laboratories, and a number of other pharmaceutical companies are also heavily involved in nanotechnology. The reason, according to Mike Roco, senior adviser for nanotechnology at the National Science Foundation, is that half of all pharmaceuticals by 2010 will be developed by nanotechnology, a point the next few chapters will elaborate on. Ireland-based Elan Pharmaceutical has publicly stated that it is using a proprietary technology called NanoCrystals to speed up the delivery time of an over-the-counter painkiller from three hours to less than twenty minutes, and Advectus Life Sciences claims that in studies its nanoparticles have shown promise in the treatment of brain tumors.

The most promising sign that the United States industrial sector is awakening to the potential and importance of nanotechnology is the establishment, in late 2001, of the NanoBusiness Alliance, a consortium of business and government leaders dedicated to advancing the development of nanotechnology in the United States. Chaired by former Speaker of the House Newt Gingrich, the board of the alliance also includes luminaries such as Mike Roco and Steve Jurvetson, a leading venture capitalist for the firm Draper Fisher Jurvetson.

Other large U.S. companies involved in nanotechnology include DuPont, Dow, GE, Honeywell, Motorola, Amgen, Rockwell Scientific Company, Lockheed Martin, Exxon, Sun Microsystems, Texas Instruments, Intel, Corning, Engelhard, Goodrich, Cabot, Xerox, Applied Materials, Raytheon, Eastman Kodak, and 3M. One company, Hybrid Plastics, is already delivering nanostructured chemicals to more than two hundred customers, including Intel, JDS Uniphase, Boeing, and Estée Lauder.

Other global companies, including BASF, Siemens, Henkel-Chemie, Hoechst, Degussa, and Samsung are also involved in nanotechnology. The markets they are looking at span the spectrum from tires, paints, printing inks, coatings, and plastics to ultrafast computers, new drugs, and advanced communication technologies.

Most automotive companies are also investing in nanotechnology, including Daimler-Chrysler, Volkswagen, Toyota, and General Motors, which announced in 2001 that a number of its cars were going to be equipped with a new high-performance nanocomposite that was lightweight, scratch-resistant and rust-proof. According to one National Science Foundation official, current nanotechnology applications have the potential to save four hundred million gallons of gas annually and emit eleven billion fewer pounds of carbon dioxide into the air.

Presently only a few publicly traded pure-play nano-technology companies exist. Nanophase Corporation, located outside of Chicago, is a leader in manufacturing nanoparticles, and among its customers are BASF, the U.S. Navy, and an undisclosed major automotive manufacturer that is using nanoparticles in two of its models to enhance combustion. Altair Nanotechnologies, another publicly traded company, is also specializing in nanoparticles, although its intended market is reported to be the potentially lucrative fuel cell and battery industries. A third company is Veeco Instruments, which specializes in atomic force microscopes.

Equally—and perhaps more—significant developments are taking place all around the globe in the multitude of promising nanotechnology start-ups that are springing up on an almost daily basis. This naturally leads us to the venture-capital market, which serves as a good indicator of where a technology stands in relation to the market. Most venture capitalists only invest in those companies that show the potential to transform a promising technology into a commercial product within eighteen to twenty-four months.

VENTURE CAPITAL

By the end of 2003, Steve Jurvetson expects 40 percent of the companies he funds to be in the field of nanotechnology. In fact, his firm is so impressed with the potential of the field that it has already invested in eight nanotech companies. They are not alone. According to the Nano-Business Alliance, the amount invested by venture capitalists in nanotechnology companies will increase to $1.2 billion by the end of 2003, up 1,200 percent from the $100 million invested in 1999.

Lux Capital, based in New York, is among the firms trying to carve out a niche in nanotechnology funding. In August 2001, they published "The Nanotechnology Report," an in-depth look at the technology and the people and companies spurring its development. CMP Científica, an international nanotechnology consultancy, is also staking out ground as a leader in the field and published "The Nanotechnology Opportunity Report" in March 2002. (The reports are not for the faint of heart. They retail for $4,700 and $1,995, respectively). Ardesta LLC is also aggressively moving into the area. While its horizon is broader than nanotechnology (it also includes MEMS), a substantial portion of its $100 million fund will be invested in emerging nanotechnology companies. The company is also the sponsor of an excellent website, smalltimes.com, and a monthly magazine. Readers interested in staying abreast of daily developments in nanotechnology are strongly encouraged to use these resources.

Nanotechnology, in a sign that it is picking up cachet, has also been added to the technologies that established investment houses such as JP Morgan and Merrill Lynch are now tracking. Merrill Lynch even went so far as to produce a six-page report for its investors titled "The Next Small Thing: An Introduction to Nanotechnology" in late 2001.

The disruptive nature of technology—its ability to render billion-dollar industries obsolete—is also prompting many large companies either to create or redirect their existing venture-capital arms to add nanotechnology companies to their investment portfolios. Chevron Technology, the investment arm of Chevron, launched a $100 million fund with nanotechnology as one of its main themes in 2001. Henkel similarly created a $100 million fund, while BASF, General Electric, Mitsubishi, and Mitsui also created funds averaging close to the same figure.

By investing in these nanotechnology companies early, the large firms hope to be able to better track developments in the field and utilize those developments sooner. (One such example of this is Dow's investing in the early stages of NanoGram, a small nanotechnology start-up that has targeted the $10 billion optical-component market.) In the longer run, they also more favorably position themselves to acquire some of the companies.

The impact of all this money is hard to determine. Many of the venture-capital firms are being tight-tongued about their investments at this point. A few companies have, however, emerged.

- **Arryx,** a Chicago-based firm, which received funding from Draper Fisher Jurvetson, does nanoscale manipulation through a process called Holographic Optic Trap technology. The technology has the ability to intelligently and independently manipulate thousands of tiny objects with lasers and has a wide variety of potential uses in the biotechnology, pharmaceutical, and photonics industries.
- **Carbon Nanotechnologies,** a Houston, Texas, firm, was founded by Richard Smalley, the Nobel Prize winner in Chemistry in 1996 for his codiscovery of the buckyball. Smalley received $15 million in funding to help establish the company as a leader in the production of carbon nanotubes.
- **Molecular Imprints, Inc.,** based in Austin, Texas, secured $9.2 million in venture capital funding in February

2002 to help develop super high-resolution lithography tools that might enable a variety of high-performance applications in the semiconductor, MEMS, optical, and nanodevice industries.

- **NanoGram,** located in Fremont, California, has raised $35 million and has developed a commercial manufacturing process to produce optical amplifiers, passive planar waveguards, and waveguide lasers that will be of potential interest to the telecommunications industry.

- **NanoInk,** a Chicago-based company, secured $3 million in 2002 and intends to sell an automated suite of tools that enables customers to build structures smaller than 10 nanometers routinely and quickly. The company will achieve this by depositing molecules onto a surface through a patent-pending process called Dip Pen Nanolithography.

- **Nanomuscle** of Antioch, California, has raised close to $10 million from a variety of sources to assist in its goal of using nanotechnology-enabled shape memory alloys (materials that can change shape under different conditions) to replace small motors in toys, cameras, disk drives, printers, and automobiles.

- **NanoOpto,** located in Somerset, New Jersey, received $16 million in funding in late 2001 and an additional $4 million in 2002 and applies proprietary nano-optics and nanomanufacturing technology to design and manufacture components for optical networking.

- **Nanosphere, Inc.** of Northbrook, Illinois, has received $8.5 million in funding and is seeking an additional $16 million to launch a nanoparticle array probe for genomics and proteomics research in early 2003 and a clinical diagnostic system by 2005.

- **NanoSys,** located in both Cambridge, Massachusetts, and Palo Alto, California, secured $1.7 million in 2002 and has developed proprietary technology that can manufacture a wide variety of products, including nanowires, nanosensors, and hybrid plastic solar cells. Any one of these products, if successful, could revolutionize industries as large and diverse as semiconductors, health care, telecommunications, and energy.

- **Ntera,** an Irish-based company developing nanomaterials used to manufacture "paper-quality" displays, received $5 million in funding from Cross Atlantic Capital Partners. Potential applications of their products include in-store pricing systems, advertising signage, mobile communications, electronic papers and books, and photovoltaic cells. The company also announced an agreement with Merck reportedly worth billions over the coming decade. It is likely that Merck was impressed with applications of their nanostructured materials for medical diagnostic sensors and drug delivery.

- **Nantero,** a Massachusetts-based company, received $6 million from a handful of venture-capital firms that believe the company's ability to build a high-density nonvolatile random access memory using nanotechnology has the potential to operate substantially faster than existing DRAM (dynamic random access memory) technology and will allow for "instant-on" computers. The memory market is a $100 billion annual industry, so if Nantero can capture even a small portion of the market, reaching a market capitalization greater than $1 billion is a real possibility.

- **Quantum Dot Corporation,** located in Hayward, California, secured an undisclosed amount of venture-capital funding and is creating unique nanocrystals that fluoresce different colors and can be tagged to a variety of nanoscale agents, like DNA. These "dots" will allow medical researchers to better understand molecular interactions (such as why some healthy cells allow viruses in and others don't) and then provide pharmaceutical researchers the ability to test and see how a variety of drugs work to counteract diseases and viruses.

- **ZettaCore,** based in Denver, Colorado, has also received an undisclosed amount of funding and is developing ultradense, low-power molecular memory chips that have the potential to revolutionize the microelectronics industry. The company is working to use molecules to store massive amounts of information for long periods of time using relatively little power.
- **Zyvex Corporation,** a Dallas start-up founded by James Von Ehr, a true believer in the vast economic potential of nanotechnology, received a $25 million National Institute for Standards and Technology (NIST) grant to help develop the nanoscale equipment that will be necessary for future nanotechnology developments.

The result of the billions of dollars that governments, big businesses, and venture-capital firms are pouring into nanotechnology, as well as the "sweat equity" of the scientists, researchers, and entrepreneurs, is confirmation that the science is real, the near-term business applications are real, and the business prospects are bright. In the words of Steve Jurvetson, "It's starting to happen!"

NANOPOINTS

* Is there government-related nanotechnology research that your company should be aware of? Is someone in your company responsible for tracking these developments?
* Are there opportunities for your company to collaborate with nanotechnology-related research that is occurring at a university near you?

* Does the trade association you belong to monitor developments in nanotechnology? If not, can an organization like the new NanoBusiness Alliance help you?
* Do you have a method for tracking venture-capital investments in "disruptive" nanotechnology companies that, if successful, could threaten your business?

CHAPTER FOUR

Today: Nanotechnology Establishes a Foothold

"NANOTECHNOLOGY IS A HIGH TECH WAVE THAT'S BEGINNING TO SWEEP THE WORLD. . . . THE WORLD IS GOING NANO."

—CHAD MIRKIN

If you need more proof that the nano revolution isn't far off, read this chapter. By the end of 2003, computer memory will have improved forty times over the previous year's capability, crystal-clear thirty-two-inch flat panel displays will make your current TV look fat, slow, and dim in comparison, and two separate nanotechnology-related products will be able to render anthrax harmless. Nanotechnology is, in fact, *already* changing a variety of businesses. Most of them, to be honest, are quite ordinary. Vinyl flooring, windows, coatings, mirrors, drill bits, tennis balls, lubricants, skin creams, printers, catalysts, plastics, toys, and khaki pants might not sound particularly sexy or high tech, but they are at the cutting edge of massive change. More important, they are providing companies, big and small alike, with a distinct advantage *today*. This chapter will reveal what nano-innovations your company can use right now to become a leader in your industry.

MILLIPEDE AND COMPUTER MEMORY

In 1956, IBM shipped the world's first disk drive. It held five megabytes and had to be delivered on a truck because it was the size of a refrigerator. Forty-five years later, IBM was still a player in the disk-drive market—although its original refrigerator/disk had shrunk to 2.5 inches and could store one million times more information. In 2002, however, IBM sold a large share of its business to a competitor, Hitachi. Most analysts viewed it as a classic business failure—a large company too inflexible to keep up in a competing market. Few viewed it as the savvy, strategic, and bold bet on a disruptive new technology that it really is.

In late 2003, IBM will formally announce Millipede, a new data-storage device capable of storing approximately one terabit (one hundred billion bytes) of data per square inch. The device, which resembles a walking millipede when it is operational, consists of a thousand nano-sized probes placed on a silicon chip. These probes are then pointed at another layer of silicon laminated with a polymer, individually heated, and poked into the polymer to make nano-indentations. These indentations can then be read as bits of information. Think of it as a Braille reader that decodes molecule-sized bumps.

Millipede will have storage capacity forty times greater than devices available in early 2002, will be able to access information much quicker, and will use significantly less power. The devices, because they are small, will find immediate uses in cell phones, laptops, personal digital assistants, digital cameras, and MP3 players.

The implications are that business representatives will be able to hold more information on their computers and provide customers better demonstrations of their products. Doctors will be able to maintain more patient information in their PDAs, and tourists will no longer need to carry any film or disks—even if they take hundreds of photos over the course of a three-week trip to Europe. Filmmakers and film developers alike will see their business erode further as the advantages of digital technology are enhanced by this nanotech-enabled advance in memory.

IBM's technology is, however, in its infancy. New polymers might allow the company to place even more nano-indentations per square inch (up to 500 gigabytes), and the company believes it has the potential to improve the number of nano-sized probes from over one thousand to one million. At such a level, doctors will be capable not only of holding all of their patient information, but they will have the capability of cross-referencing that information against vast databases of existing medical information. Faster and better diagnosis of disease is just one of the technology's many promising applications.

The legal industry will also undergo significant change. If massive volumes of state and federal statutes as well as case law can be stored on computers, the need for legal assistants and paralegals, who spend a lot of time doing research, will decrease. As database-mining software and computers both increase in sophistication and power, these professions will be squeezed even further.

Every medical and law school that profits from educating these professionals will also need to rethink its core business as both the number of students and their needs change. For example, in the past, doctors were trained to memorize copious amounts of information and then, through a process of questioning their patients, apply that knowledge to make a diagnosis. With the amount of medical information doubling every few years, this system no longer makes sense—especially since the technology exists, in the form of more powerful computer memories, for the doctors to carry much of the information with them. Those institutions that recognize this reality and take the lead in developing new tools and methodologies for training students are likely to be the leaders in tomorrow's educational world.

Companies specializing in database management and database mining will also need to evaluate how more powerful computer memory can be exploited. Similarly any business or service-provider that relies on service and repair manuals to conduct its business can benefit from this advancement by transitioning away from large, paper-based manuals, which are expensive to update and cumbersome to carry. Many airlines are, in fact, already transitioning away from large paper manuals—which pilots use to calculate how much fuel is required for a given passenger/cargo load—because they are causing some pilots back injuries and because their weight is, ironically, contributing to higher fuel costs. (While the manual may weigh only ten pounds, this weight multiplied by thousands of flights adds up to major fuel costs.)

IBM is reportedly working on new market applications for this technology as well as new products. Just what these new applications and products are is not known, but the smart business executive must stay abreast of developments to see if the new product might disrupt existing businesses.

IBM is not the only company playing in the computer-memory market. Nantero of Woburn, Massachusetts, is working with carbon nanotubes to construct active memory elements that will enable "always on" computers, while Denver-based ZettaCore is developing organic molecules to function as memory. Hewlett-Packard is working diligently to develop an Atomic Resolution Storage product that could encode one bit per atom. If successful, this device would allow for the storage of material at one hundred million times the density of current disks.

To understand what these developments might mean, consider this: Since 1988, the price of storing one megabyte (one million bytes) of information has fallen from $11.54 per megabyte to less than one cent. With IBM's Millipede, this could change to one gigabyte (one thousand megabytes) per penny, Nantero or ZettaCore could increase this density to one terabyte (one thousand gigabytes) a penny, and Hewlett-Packard could potentially increase it to one petabyte (one thousand terabytes) per penny.

CARBON NANOTUBES

Data-storage technology is not the only technology feeling the cold, hard impact of the nano revolution. In 2002, Applied Nanotech (Austin, Texas) demonstrated a fourteen-inch nanotube display (comparable to a TV or computer screen) using a low-cost fabrication technique. By December of 2003, Samsung is expected to have on store shelves a thirty-two-inch carbon nanotube flat panel display. The screen will be so clear that it will be visible from any angle in a room, so bright it will be visible even in direct sunlight, and so crisp that the human eye will eventually not be able to distinguish the resolution because it is so fine.

The implication is that a few grams of carbon nanotubes (costing just a few dollars) are going to begin replacing the cathode-ray tubes that are in most television screens today. When presented with a product that is thinner, lighter, brighter, and uses less energy and has a clearer picture, it is difficult to imagine how the plasma and cathode-ray tube industries—and even high-definition television (HDTV)—will compete.

By 2004, it is quite possible that screens on computers and PDA's will also start going to carbon nanotubes. The effect goes beyond just better pictures. The additional space that is freed up due to thinner screens will allow even more room for memory, further multiplying the already noted effect of increased memory capacity.

Surgical, military, and automotive devices will also likely begin employing flat panel displays based on carbon nanotubes. The reason: Clearer pictures will allow doctors, pilots, and drivers to perform their tasks better, while using significantly less energy.

Not all of carbon nanotubes' impact is so dramatic. Nanoledge, a French start-up, is now using them in a brand of tennis rackets to make them stronger and lighter. Initially the product will not pose a significant threat to most tennis-racket manufacturers, but as the price comes down and the product begins to confer a unique advantage to its user, it will.

NANOPARTICLES: "NEW AND IMPROVED" PRODUCTS

Nanophase Technologies Corporation, based in Romeoville, Illinois, is currently producing nanoparticles that are being used in vinyl flooring. What makes the flooring so special is the nanoparticle coating. The nanoparticles are so tough that they make the product difficult to scratch and are so small that they are invisible to the naked eye (remember, the nanoparticles in sunscreens, which Nanophase also manufactures, are smaller than the wavelength of ultraviolet light). These properties allow the makers of the vinyl to offer a glossy product that can rival the look of tile, and they can offer a lifetime guarantee against rips and scratches. As a result, the flooring is taking market share away from tile manufacturers and quite likely is reducing the workload of professional tile installers.

If vinyl flooring can be given a lifetime guarantee today, it stands to reason that roofing shingles, tabletop counters, and a host of other products might also be given similar guarantees in the near future. If so, what happens to the production level of roofing shingles and tabletop counters? And what about the number of contractors needed to install these products if fewer of the existing ones are wearing out?

Another company, Cerax Nanowax, is manufacturing nanoparticle-enhanced coatings that are being used to increase the speed and control of skis and snowboards. The ultrathin coating, just a few atoms in depth, lasts significantly longer than conventional waxes because it bonds better with the composite material and because the nanoparticles were tailor-made to be water-repellent. This prevents ice from adhering to the ski and keeps the base of the ski and snowboard free of buildup.

Although Nanowax is primarily used by Olympic-caliber skiers, this is little reason to ignore it. Nanotechnology products often find their first niche in those areas where people and companies are willing to pay a premium for even a small advantage. In an Olympic sport like downhill skiing, where less than one one-hundredth of a second can separate the gold medal winner from the bronze medalist, the advantage for using a nano-enhanced material is obvious: superior performance. Businesses interested in tracking possible product applications would be wise to monitor elite sporting events such as the Olympics, NASCAR, the Tour de France, and the America's Cup.

Two more applications for nanoparticles are the printer and copier markets. Hewlett-Packard is presently working on its Cook 1 printer, which is expected to reach the market in late 2003 and will be capable of dispersing vast amounts of nanoparticles (actually nanoliters of fluid) to improve the speed, resolution, and color range of today's best printers. Xerox, on the other hand, is working on similar technology only for the copier market.

But not all applications revolve around superior performance alone. Many nanoparticles will also make products easier to maintain and more convenient to use. Nanogate, a German company, is employing nanoparticles in sinks and toilets to make them scratch- and stain-resistant, suggesting that the manufacturers of both stainless steel and bathroom cleaners should expect to feel the competitive pressure of these new particles. SuNyx (Cologne, Germany), United Kingdom-based Pilkington, and PPG Industries of Pittsburgh are all making self-cleaning windows by coating windows with nanoparticles that either won't let dirt and water particles adhere to them or, alternatively, react with dirt to dissolve it. Conservatories and homes and buildings with skylights will likely be among the first to install self-cleaning windows. However, as businesses such as the Mall of America, which must clean 1,500 glass doors a day, begin to calculate the labor and supply costs of these activities, the technology is likely to gain traction.

By the end of 2003, it is very likely that even the toy industry will be feeling the impact of nanotechnology. NanoMuscle of Antioch, California, is reportedly preparing to provide Hasbro with millions of "nanomuscles" (micron-sized devices that are created with unique nanocrystals that can change shape—and thus create motion—when applied with electrical current) for a still-classified toy due on store shelves by Christmas 2003. Businesses tempted to dismiss the technology because it is employed in the toy industry shouldn't. The nanomuscle is so strong that it has a reasonable chance of replacing a wide variety of small motors. Considering that the average home already has fifty small motors (in everything from your refrigerator to your home computer) and the average car has more than one hundred, the potential is significant.

Nanoparticles are not, however, just the playground of private enterprise. The U.S. Air Force is developing nanolubricants that have been demonstrated to operate at significantly higher temperatures than traditional lubricants (the nanoparticles don't melt or become sticky until they reach a much higher temperature), and it is also adding copper nanoparticles to motor oil to reduce engine wear. The developments, if successful, are something that any manufacturing company that uses machinery equipment and processes will want to know about.

The Navy is presently employing nanoparticle technology to coat turbines and engine parts. The heat-resistant and lubricating properties of various nanoparticles, which are applied by thermal sprays, help parts to function more efficiently and break down less often. Therefore, in addition to superior performance and the upfront cost savings associated with greater efficiency, even larger savings are accumulating due to a significant reduction in operation and maintenance schedules. This, in turn, has the potential to increase the morale of the sailors (who have to perform fewer tedious and menial tasks), yield greater productivity, and possibly increase the Navy's retention rate.

Corrosion-resistant nanoparticle coatings are also being applied to the hulls of Navy ships to reduce drag, increase speed, and reduce rust. Corrosion is estimated to cost U.S. businesses $100 billion annually, suggesting that the application of nonoxidizing nanoparticles to a variety of materials might improve a company's bottom line. Nanoparticle coatings are also being used to create a surface that makes it hard for barnacles and tube worms to adhere to hulls. If successful, the coating is expected to increase fuel efficiency of every Navy ship by 10 percent. Considering that the Navy spends $75,000 a day to power a conventional aircraft carrier, the potential savings are obvious. Further consider that 98 percent of world trade (4.5 billion metric tons a year) is carried by sea, and the implications for the massive global shipping industry are also clear.

NANOPARTICLES: AS CATALYSTS

Nanoparticles, because of their size, also make great catalysts. Catalysis, the act of using an external material to initiate, speed up, or modify a process, is the basis of a multibillion-dollar industry and is one of the more important technologies of the modern era. It plays an essential role in everything from refining oil to creating nylon to cleaning up automobile emissions to manufacturing drugs and producing fertilizers. It even gives margarine its "spreadability." New nanoparticles, manufactured to precise specifications, are allowing vastly greater efficiencies in these processes (because less material is required to produce the same result) and providing the opportunity for the creation of new products and processes. The potential savings from new and improved catalysis in the $450 billion U.S. chemical industry alone is staggering. For example, according to DuPont's 2001 annual report, the company adjusted one of its processes—and it has more than two hundred others—and saved $26 million.

As makers of nanoparticles have reduced their cost and modified the properties of the nanoparticles, entirely new markets have opened. For instance, the Japanese company Nippon is now coating mirrors on high-end automobiles with water-repellent titanium dioxide nanoparticles. The application means that antifogging mirrors are now possible. As the price of these nanoparticles continues to drop, these mirrors, which now command a premium price, will become commonplace not just in bathrooms and locker rooms around the world, but on eyeglasses and any other product where water is unwelcome.

The company is also working with titanium dioxide nanoparticles to develop other unique properties in the particles. Titanium dioxide is a well-known photocatalyst, meaning that it can react with light. One immediate application is in hospital operating rooms to react with and burn off potentially dangerous bacteria. In addition to the huge benefits of reducing the possibility of infectious disease (and potentially saving lives), the nanoparticles might have the more mundane effect of reducing the need for toxic, costly cleaners. Therefore, it can also help lessen the number of hours hospital janitors will be required to sanitize operating rooms. A cost-conscious hospital might be able to employ such material to reduce patients' exposure to various infectious diseases as well as reduce annual operational and maintenance costs.

Titanium dioxide can also photocatalytically react with sunlight to slowly break down and loosen dirt and smudges from material. Thus the idea of self-cleaning lights and appliances is not only a possibility, it is a reality. The implications are both small and large. On the smaller scale, the makers of paper towels may see their profits decline as fewer people use their products to clean little streaks on the refrigerator. And parents, especially those with young children, might actually be able to spend less time cleaning.

On the larger end of things, in Japan, Toto, Ltd. is marketing titanium dioxide-coated building tiles. Buildings with these tiles will not require annual washings and will never have to be painted. If 40 percent of the $17 billion paint industry's business comes from commercial projects, self-cleaning tiles could do serious damage to the industry. And if automobile manufacturers begin coating their new cars with self-cleaning nanoparticles, the number of independent car washes will diminish, as will the profits that gas stations currently derive from car-wash operations.

If such businesses wish to prosper, it is not too soon to begin thinking of new alternative services or products to distinguish themselves. An example of how they might be required to rethink their business can be found in how eyewear and contact lens manufacturers are being forced to rethink their business in light of the growing popularity of laser surgery. As more people opt for the corrective surgery, to maintain market share a number of eyewear manufacturers have taken to marketing eyeglasses less as a necessity and more as a style accessory. Similarly, Accuvue, a large manufacturer of disposable contact lenses, has recently begun advertising disposable contacts not for the purpose of enhancing vision but as a simple cosmetic feature to change the color of your eye.

The point is that nanoparticles are being employed today and are creating change in a number of industries and professions. And it's not just in the industrial hardware fields. Countries and cosmetic companies alike are using nanoparticles. For example, researchers in Hong Kong and Japan are experimenting with titanium dioxide nanoparticles in concrete as a way to fight pollution. In tests, the material has removed up to 90 percent of nitrogen oxide (a pollutant that is caused by diesel trucks and older cars and is a major contributor to acid rain and smog), suggesting that polluted cities might be able to combat serious health issues by embedding these nanoparticles directly into their streets and buildings.

Another company, Technanogy, is producing nanoaluminum particles to be used as a fuel additive for the space shuttle. The smaller size and, by design, the greater surface area of nanoparticles (remember, more of their atoms are in direct contact with the surface) have been shown to produce a thirtyfold increase in the combustion rate in solid rockets. The increased power will help lower the cost of launching material into space and bring the goal of commercial space development one step closer to reality. And if NASA can use these particles today, they can potentially be used by the major automotive manufacturers tomorrow to increase fuel efficiency. Manufacturers of pyrotechnics and munitions can also use nanoparticles to improve product performance.

NANOPARTICLES: COSMETICS AND MEDICAL ENHANCEMENT

L'Oréal and Lancôme are even using nanoparticles in skin creams and hair conditioners. The tiny size of the particles can be precisely controlled to determine how deep the creams penetrate, and, based on the physical composition of the nanoparticle, it can be made to do different things, including removing dirt and oil or moisturizing skin or hair to precise specifications. The impact of these developments is already being felt in the $20 billion cosmetics industry.

Novavax, located in Columbia, Maryland, is using nanoparticle technology to develop a skin-absorbent estrogen lotion that reduces hot flashes and other symptoms in menopausal women. Such a lotion could replace the drug Premarin, the third-most-prescribed drug in America, responsible for close to $1 billion in sales. If a lotion developed using nanoparticle technology can replace this drug, the entire pharmaceutical industry may need to rethink a sizable portion of its business. (In addition, Premarin, which takes its name from its main source, pregnant mare urine, is often criticized by animal rights activists who are concerned with the treatment of horses. This demonstrates that nanotechnology might also offer consumers more ethically attractive treatments in addition to more effective products.)

Another company, Nanoscale Materials, located in Manhattan, Kansas, has introduced two new nanocrystal products. One is a skin cream that will provide instant protection against anthrax and other chemical agents, and the other is a spray applied from a fire extinguisher-type device that reportedly interacts with anthrax molecules (in an undisclosed manner) and renders the biological agent harmless. The usefulness of such a product, especially in light of the anthrax scares in the fall of 2001, is obvious.

While the more immediate applications will rightly concentrate on addressing national-security needs and bioterrorism threats, there is no reason to believe that if nanocrystals can render anthrax harmless, they won't also be able to work on less pressing issues such as acne or halitosis. If so, the $550 million U.S. market for acne products and the $766 million mouthwash industry had better stay abreast of developments in this field.

Many of the major pharmaceutical companies, including Genentech, Roche, and GlaxoSmithKline, are using nanocrystals (similar in nature to nanoparticles) to "tag" molecules. After constructing nanocrystals with unique binding properties and either specific magnetic qualities, fluorescent characteristics, or sizes, researchers can then attach these nanocrystals to molecules and monitor them to see how cells and proteins and other biological agents interact (magnetic sensors can follow nanocrystals made of metallic properties, and lasers can illuminate nanocrystals calibrated so different sizes respond with different colors). This knowledge, in turn, is providing the researchers with a better understanding of the complex cellular changes and the events associated with various diseases. The result is that these nanocrystals will aid in the faster discovery of new drugs and the faster diagnosis of diseases.

By incorporating nanocrystals, which are water-soluble and dissolve more easily in the body than bigger particles, any medicine that now takes a long time to address the condition of a patient may be positively impacted by nanotechnology because the medication will take effect sooner.

CREATING NANOMATERIALS

In addition to capitalizing on the unique nanoparticle properties of size and composition, scientists are now also adding nanoparticles to existing materials or forming them into new materials. The result is that nanotech is now infiltrating the vast world of material science.

The clothing industry will be the first to be revolutionized. Nano-Tex, LLC, a unit of Burlington Industries, is helping Lee Jeans and Eddie Bauer produce a new line of jeans and khakis with nanomaterials that resist stains. Nano-sized whiskers protrude from the fabric, allowing any spill to be easily wiped away without lasting damage to the fabric. In addition to disrupting the $4 billion khaki market and the $5 billion blue-jean industry, detergent companies, dry cleaners, and laundromats might also begin losing market share as these nanomaterials become more prevalent in all types of clothing.

The implications of this material, while currently directed toward the clothing industry, are not, however, limited to that sector. Any number of materials can be manufactured with nanoparticles, including carpets, furniture, and window coverings. If such materials can withstand wear and tear better and prove more resistant to staining, the potential to accrue savings is significant for the $92 billion hospitality and restaurant industry, whose many products suffer from overuse and abuse. Furthermore, businesses currently supplying the hospitality industry with carpets, bedding, furniture, curtains, or even cleaning materials and services might be in danger of losing business.

Another huge industry that is already being impacted by nanotechnology is the $300 billion U.S. plastics industry. Nanocor, a subsidiary of Amcol, is now producing nanoclays and nanocomposites for a variety of uses in everyday plastic products. Everything from car parts and casings to tools and toys will be affected. For example, Nanocor's nanomaterials, due to their unique molecular structure, can provide distinct advantages to packaging materials because they act as a barrier to moisture, chemical vapors, gases, and solvents. By altering the size and structure of various materials at the nanoscale, the desired molecules can be allowed in and undesirable molecules kept out. Such nanoclays are also rapidly gaining acceptance in the global plastics industry because they can easily be integrated into existing process equipment and because the price continues to drop.

The implications will be noteworthy, especially for the $480 billion global packaging industry. Any product that can be packaged in a stronger, lighter, more durable or temperature-resistant material will benefit from nanotechnology. Consider the simple beer bottle. A few years ago, the technology to store beer in plastic did not exist. Today the bottles are used in almost every major sporting stadium in the country and occupy space on almost every liquor store shelf. The material savings from using plastic instead of aluminum or glass are already significant, and the reduced transportation costs alone, derived from the lighter weight, are even more significant.

But the above savings are just the beginning. Nanoclays are now being used to make the plastic even lighter. More important, they are being used to make the plastic nearly impermeable. In essence, the nanoclays create a difficult maze for gas molecules to escape, which means it takes longer for the gas to diffuse through the container. Because of this, the shelf life of beer in a plastic bottle will increase from 120 days to an estimated 180 days and possibly even longer. This means that less money will be lost due to the product's reaching its expiration date. Furthermore, additional savings (in the form of reduced transportation and human labor costs) will accrue because less old beer will have to be returned manually to the plant. Beer distributors are thus likely to be among the first to feel the subtle and not-so-subtle effects of these nanotechnology-enhanced products.

The beer industry, however, is only one of many industries that will be impacted by these new nanomaterials. Nanocor has produced a nanocomposite material that releases herbicide in a limited, albeit constant, form to prevent roots from destroying pipes. This means that herbicide and pipe manufacturers alike will be impacted because farmers no longer need to purchase as much herbicide nor will they need to replace their irrigation pipes as often.

InMat, LLC is producing a nanocomposite that allows tennis balls to keep their proper bounce for twice as long. Wilson Sporting Goods is now manufacturing the new nanocomposite ball, which was the official ball of the 2002 Davis Cup. As the price of the ball drops, pro shops around the world may begin to notice a remarkable decline in the number of tennis balls they are selling because the old balls will stay good longer.

In 2001, General Motors installed running boards constructed of nanocomposite materials on models of Safari and Astro minivans. In addition to being lighter, the nanocomposites are significantly more resistant to wear and tear. While one lighter part will not lead to significantly better gas mileage, as more parts—including body panels, timing belts, and engine covers—are manufactured with nanomaterials, the saving will begin to accumulate. Toyota is reportedly already employing a nanocrystalline steel in some of its models.

Nanodyne, located in New Brunswick, New Jersey, has been producing superstrong drill bits manufactured out of nanostructured tungsten carbide that doubles the hardness of its parts and significantly extends the product's life. Considering that many of today's strongest alloys are only crudely controlled at the molecular level (meaning that there are more defects in the material, which in turn limits its strength), the opportunity to produce stronger, lighter, and more unique materials is here today. Cars, planes, buildings, machine parts, and hundreds of other existing commercial products can all be improved with the aid of new nanomaterials right now. This will be particularly true as the price of the nanomaterials becomes cost-competitive.

It is likely that the price will come down for the simple reason that economies of scale of production will drive them down. As the price of carbon nanotubes, nanoparticles, and nanomaterials reach commodity-pricing level, thousands of other applications become possible. Consider the following example. A unique, high-end nanometal powder, like that reportedly produced by NanoPowder, a company located in Israel, might filter through the economy like this: The nanoscale powder, which is embedded in a polymer composite to give the material the radiation-shielding properties of a metal but the lightness of plastic, will first be targeted for space-related applications. (The company is, in fact, working on such an application.) NASA, which currently spends between $10,000 and $20,000 to launch a pound of material into space, will be willing to pay for the more expensive nanomaterial because it reduces, by a few hundred pounds, the weight of the space shuttle.

The increased production of the powder and consequent decline in price has reached the point where Boeing and Airbus are funding research and considering incorporating the nanometal and other nanotechnology into the production of their next generation of jumbo jets (because their customers, the major airlines, are all demanding more fuel-efficient aircraft). The nanopowder will at some point drop to the price point where it can be profitably incorporated into their jets. This increased production will further reduce the price to the point where it is available for higher-end automobiles like Jaguar or Lexus. Over the next five years, the material will be in moderately priced cars and will eventually become commonplace. The lesson here is that while a steel, aluminum, or composite company might be able to afford the loss of a few hundred pounds of business to NASA, it can ill afford to lose the automobile market.

This might sound unlikely, but according to the Hitachi Research Institute, the market for nanomaterials alone is estimated to reach $340 billion by 2011, and more than one hundred companies are currently producing or developing nanomaterials.

The bottom line is that nanotechnology is here today, and it is only going to become more pronounced in the future. If an old, well-established company like IBM can risk a huge portion of its business on a new technology, can you? More important, can you afford *not* to?

NANOPOINTS

* Do you have equipment and parts that might benefit from an improved coating?
* Would your operation and maintenance schedules change if certain equipment parts didn't have to be checked and/or cleaned as often?
* Does your business supply either products or services to industries that might employ nanomaterials? If so, is it possible that the demand for your product might decrease?
* Are you considering any major renovation or building projects? If so, are there nanomaterials (e.g., "smart windows" or "smart tiles") that could be employed to produce significant long-term savings?
* Do you have products that might benefit from a material with a better strength-to-weight ratio?
* Do you have packaging requirements that might benefit from improved properties?
* Are you asking for bids from new suppliers so that you will be aware of these products?
* Are entirely new products available to you based on new materials?

CHAPTER FIVE

2004 & 2005: Faster, Smaller, Cheaper, Better

"NANOTECHNOLOGY IS GOING TO BLOSSOM AND
TURN INTO A MAJOR FORCE IN SCIENCE OVER THE
NEXT TWO YEARS. . . . IT'S ALMOST A RUNAWAY
FREIGHT TRAIN, THERE IS SO MUCH EXCITEMENT
OVER IT."

—CHAD MIRKIN

In 1930, a three-minute telephone call between London and New York City cost $244 and required the caller to go to a special location to make the call. In 1990, the same call cost $3.32 and could be conducted in the comfort of one's home or office. Today, the call costs less than a dollar and can literally be made almost anywhere from a cell phone. Such is the nature of technological progress.

The application of technological progress has not, however, been evenly spread over all industries. For example, if the automobile had followed the same rate of progression that the computer has made over the last fifty years in terms of providing ever-greater power at a lower cost, every car on the road today would have almost unlimited gas mileage and cost only a few pennies. Similarly, progress in the pharmaceutical industry would not have been limited to the introduction of one or two major blockbuster drugs a year—drugs that took a decade to get to the marketplace and cost $500 million to $800 million to develop.

By 2004, a variety of diseases will be better understood, including Lou Gehrig's disease, cystic fibrosis, and Alzheimer's, which affects four million Americans according to the National Institutes of Health. New disease-detection methods will allow many types of cancer, including ovarian, to be diagnosed earlier.

Understanding how proteins fold will help pharmaceutical companies improve the prediction of molecular interactions, increase their ability to design effective drugs, and reduce the amount of trial and error required for developing a new drug.

The cascade of new drugs will also force doctors to stay more apprised of the latest treatments. Even those medical professionals who might have been resistant to using more powerful PDAs (brought to us by nanotechnology) will be forced to employ these devices because it is quite likely that the base level of medical knowledge and treatments available will surpass the capacity of even the most intelligent doctors to remember which drugs—or which combination of drugs—is most effective—no matter how many conferences they attend or professional journals they read. (Note: Access to more complete patient and drug information might also prevent some malpractice lawsuits as fewer treatments are misprescribed to patients.)

The impact of nanotechnology on drug discovery is broader than just the health-care industry. If the protein amyloid, which has been found to clog the brains of Alzheimer's patients, can be better understood, a treatment for this debilitating illness might be found. In addition to extending the productive life of thousands of people, the new treatment will also relieve untold amounts of pain and anguish suffered by the children and spouses of Alzheimer's victims. It might also significantly reduce the patient load of the 17,000 nursing homes across the country. This is especially true as America's 76 million baby-boomers begin to grow older. The $600 billion long-term-care industry and the burgeoning long-term health-care-insurance industry will need to begin factoring these changes into their strategic-planning processes today. Everything from the numbers of beds required to the monthly premium rate for long-term insurance will need to be revisited.

DISEASE DETECTION

An increased understanding of the human genome (genomics), coupled with more powerful computers and a greater understanding of proteins (an emerging field of science known as proteomics that evaluates the composition, structure, and interactions of proteins), will all contribute to improved disease detection. These improvements will help identify sooner both characteristic disease proteins and DNA "markers," signs that indicate that an individual may be predisposed to a cancer or other diseases. Finding the DNA markers or proteins will allow victims of genetic diseases to take preventative steps much sooner.

For example, ovarian cancer, which kills an estimated 14,000 women every year (according to the NIH), is not usually diagnosed until it has reached the very late stages. Although there are tests available now that determine the presence of a protein typical of ovarian cancer, these tests may be inaccurate and require supplementation with other diagnostic methods.

The insurance industry will again be among the first to feel the impact from these advances. A current example: If a DNA marker for breast cancer, BRCA2, is found in a patient (perhaps very early in that person's life), should that person receive treatment even though the marker may have only a 50 percent correlation with the cancer? When will medical screening be permissible? What will insurance companies and employers be able to do with that information? When will medical services have to be provided and at what cost? These are just a few of the questions that the insurance industry, concerned individuals and businesses, and public policymakers are struggling with today regarding breast cancer. The issues involved with these illnesses will only increase with improved diagnostic capabilities. The positive aspect of these developments is that the early diagnoses of many diseases will reduce the treatment cost, duration, and invasiveness for the patient. Conversely, manufacturers of diagnostic equipment and suppliers of chemotherapy treatments will need to rethink their business model as treatment moves from curing a disease to preventing it.

But perhaps the greatest boon to disease detection will be nanosensors. Nanosphere, a company located outside of Chicago, reports that within the 2004 to 2005 time frame it will have a detection system on the market that employs nanosensors to detect the presence of anthrax, smallpox, and a variety of illnesses ten times faster than anything on the market today and 100,000 times more accurately. The system, which Nanosphere hopes to deploy in a hand-held device, uses DNA strands that match and bind with a patient's DNA to test for hundreds (or thousands) of different agents. In many ways, it is a nano-sized lock-and-key system, where the idea is to have a surface with many different keys on it. The patient's DNA, or "locks," are applied to the surface. The approach is to determine how many locks have been opened. Nanosphere is not the only company working on such a device. Agilent, Motorola, SurroMed, Molecular Nanosystems, Danish-based Cantion, and Berlin-based Scienion are a few of the others working on similar technology. And while it is not known at this time *which* company or companies will win the battle in the marketplace, nanosensors are a disruptive technology that will impact a number of industries and professions.

If the price (which is not known at this time) of this laboratory diagnostic equipment continues to drop as expected, it is entirely possible that doctors will have such equipment on their desktops within a few years. This suggests that the makers and suppliers of expensive laboratories and laboratory equipment will be adversely affected. If a simple, easy-to-use device can quickly run a test for not just one virus but for hundreds or even thousands, the need to send material to a lab will decrease. It stands to reason then that the number of medical lab technicians conducting these tests will also diminish. If this occurs, those academic institutions training medical lab technicians will need to revisit both how many people they should be training and what they should be training them to do.

Everything from E. coli and salmonella (which affects an estimated 3.8 million Americans a year) to foot-and-mouth disease and anthrax, which have imposed significant costs on Britain and the U.S., respectively, from 2001–2003, will be detected at a much earlier stage with these new nanosensors. Officials responsible for airport security and border crossings will also have enhanced tools to counter bioterrorism. For example, Michael Tailor at the University of California at San Diego is using nanomaterials to develop a network of sensors to detect poison gases such as sarin. (Such sensors could be strategically placed throughout a subway system or outside the White House to pick up even the slightest hint of a deadly agent.) Other antiterrorism applications for nanosensors are at water-treatment centers or reservoirs—anywhere a large quantity of water is stored. The same is true for air-intake systems for large buildings, government facilities, or sports arenas. The nanosensors could, because of their sensitivity, generate an alarm if even small amounts of toxins were detected.

The applications go beyond prevention of terrorism. The sensors have applications anywhere a small amount of material needs to be detected. Police investigators, for instance, will be able to use nanosensors to collect forensic evidence more quickly, more easily, and more accurately. Therefore, investigators could run samples quickly before crime sites are contaminated and perhaps while the perpetrators are still in the vicinity. The scope of nanosensors even reaches beyond humans. California's $6.8 billion wine industry will benefit as crippling vine diseases are caught and eradicated at a much earlier stage with the help of supersensitive nanosensors. There are even multiple agricultural applications, where awareness of a hazard such as a crop infection in an important commodity like rice, if known early enough, can make the difference between feeding a country and starvation.

DRUG DELIVERY

Due to the nature of the health-care industry, especially the important role that the Food and Drug Administration plays in approving and regulating new drugs and new treatments, it is difficult to place precise time frames on when specific advances will be approved and find their way to market.

What we do know is that some new drugs and procedures involving nanotechnology will be in different clinical stages during 2004–2005. Among the most exciting developments is a company named C Sixty, located in Houston, Texas, which is working on a device it likens to a "molecular pincushion." The center of the pincushion is a carbon-based structure with drugs and protein detectors attached. The nanoscopic device, which can be injected into the body, can easily and precisely fit into the pocket of an AIDS virus and disrupt its ability to reproduce (a process somewhat similar to how the drug Gleevec "turns off" an enzyme that causes white blood cells to become cancerous and multiply in certain leukemia patients). The device is also a vast improvement over many of the drug-delivery platforms currently on the market because it is nontoxic and as such it does not cause the severe reactions that many of today's drug platforms do. Furthermore, these nanodevices have the benefit of being rapidly and easily modified. This is important because many of today's AIDS drugs are effective only for the short time before the virus adapts to the drug. If new drugs can be inserted into the nanodevices at will, the power of the virus to adapt and propagate is neutralized.

The immediate impact of such nanoscopic drugs, if successful, is obvious. A cure for AIDS will solve a 20-year-old quest for eliminating the deadly disease. The longer-term impact may bring less deadly issues into focus: How can we best educate the greater numbers of 15- to 25-year-old Africans who survive? If unprotected sex increases because AIDS is no longer a threat, how do we deal with a rise in the number of unintended pregnancies? From a generation of young people in Africa spared a premature death to its societal impact on the notion of casual sex, new opportunities and new problems may arise. In the shorter term, thousands of government and private-sector researchers will be freed to work in new fields, and organizations such as the Stop AIDS Project or the International HIV Organization will be able to redirect their resources and talents to new worthwhile pursuits.

Other researchers in Texas are working on a nanoscale cancer "smart bomb." The researchers are placing a single atom of the highly radioactive material actinium-225 inside a nanoscale cage made of carbon and nitrogen. They then attach to the outside of the cage a protein that adheres only to cancer cells. Once the attachment between protein and cancer cell takes place, the cage decays and the radioactive material is released and kills only the cancer cells.

Preliminary tests have shown that this smart bomb can kill leukemia, lymphoma, breast, ovarian, and prostate cancer cells. And although it has been tested only in mice, at the time of this publication, the results have shown that mice treated with the procedure have lived up to three hundred days (and have then shown no sign of cancer) compared to an average of forty-three days for those mice with cancer that did not receive the treatment. (Note: Another company, CritiTech, Inc., located in Lawrence, Kansas, is using a nanoscale version of paclitaxel, aptly named nanopaclitaxel, which has also been shown to be more effective than regular paclitaxel in treating ovarian cancer in mice.)

Another promising area of nanomedicine involves the treatment of diabetes. Tejal Desai, a leading researcher at Boston University, has created a tiny silicon box that contains pancreatic cells taken from animals. The box, which is implanted in diabetics, is surrounded by a material with very specific-size nanopores. The pores are big enough to allow glucose molecules to enter but small enough to keep harmful antibodies out. When the pancreatic cells detect too much glucose, they release insulin—whose molecules are also small enough to escape through the pores.

The impact on the treatment of diabetes—an ailment that, according to the NIH, afflicts 16 million Americans and is growing by 800,000 a year, results in 50,000 amputations per year and costs an average of $8,000 per patient a year—will be immense. Hospitals, government workers, insurance administrators, and businesses serving this huge population should all be following the developments of nanotechnology in this field.

Another company, Angstrom Medica, is developing nanocrystals of various sizes, shapes, and purity that can mix with the body's own cells to help regrow bones. The treatment of osteoporosis, which costs the U.S. healthcare system $15 billion a year and affects twenty-eight

million Americans, will be among the first areas to benefit. On the other hand, physical therapists, who serve
many of the 280,000 people who fracture their hips every
year, might lose business and therefore might have to
restructure their models of operation.

Asthma is also benefiting from nanotech. A new
nanoscale device, likened to a miniature Whiffle ball, can
encapsulate an asthma drug and help it get to the lungs
more quickly and more effectively. The result is that the
businesses that cater to the more than seventeen million
Americans who suffer from asthma will need to reexam-
ine the services and products they are offering.

Quantum Dot Corporation, located in Hayward,
California, might, within the 2004 to 2005 time frame,
completely disrupt the $2.8 billion fluorescent tagging
market. (Tagging allows researchers to track how various
drugs interact with biological agents by placing nanoscale
tags, or dots, on those agents—something larger tags cannot do due to their size.) The company's nanocrystals are
already allowing researchers to view complex interactions more clearly because the nanotags fluoresce longer
than chemical-based tags. Nanotechnology-based tags
can also be applied so that they respond with very clearly
defined bandwidths or colors of light, which allows
researchers to know exactly what they are looking at. For
example, nanoscale tags could be used to help discover
how the drug TAXOL Paclitaxel, which has proven beneficial in the treatment of cancer, is transported in cell
structures and how it reacts with the cancerous cells once
it reaches them.

The net result of all these advances in drug discovery,
disease detection, and drug delivery will be a paradigm
shift of gigantic proportions. Power will gradually shift

from the doctor to the patient. Rather than simply waiting until they are sick to throw expensive and complicated treatments at health problems, people will begin taking preventative actions much earlier and will, if necessary, be undergoing less invasive, less expensive, and ultimately more effective treatment sooner.

FUEL CELLS

Beginning in 2004, the automotive industry will begin feeling the effects of nanotechnology. Many of the impacts mentioned in the previous chapter, such as the introduction of nanocomposites into car panels and the use of nanoparticles in everything from catalytic converters to car paints, will continue. But the big change will come in the area of fuel-cell technology. Specifically nanotechnology will rapidly advance fuel cells to the point where they begin eroding the internal-combustion engine's century-old dominance of the automotive industry.

Today's car engines are only 25 percent efficient, meaning that only a quarter of the energy stored in fuel is actually converted to useful work. Fuel cells, devices that work by harnessing the chemical attraction between oxygen and hydrogen to produce electricity, are, by contrast, 50 percent efficient. Furthermore, because they use oxygen, which is taken from the air, and hydrogen, the most abundant element in the universe, they have the potential to produce energy cheaply and cleanly. Their only by-products are heat and water. The effective, efficient, and safe storage of hydrogen has, however, been the greatest obstacle to implementing the widespread use of fuel cells, and it is here that nanotechnology will play a large enabling role by creating materials strong enough to with-stand high pressures while simultaneously creating a "difficult maze" for the hydrogen atoms to escape. (Storing hydrogen is so problematic because the molecules are so small—they are .1 of a nanometer—which means they can escape through most materials, and because the amount of hydrogen necessary to fuel a car is so significant that it requires the hydrogen to be compressed at incredibly high pressures.)

Nanotechnology will also help address four other issues. In creating a fuel cell, hydrogen first needs to be harvested. Nanostructured membranes will make separating hydrogen from a variety of different sources, including gasoline, natural gas, and methanol, significantly less expensive. Graphite fibers with unique nanostructures will then increase a fuel cell's effectiveness by absorbing more hydrogen by weight, thus allowing more hydrogen to be stored in each tank. Next, nanoparticle catalysts will split hydrogen into protons and electrons with greater efficiency, thereby increasing the power of each fuel cell. And finally nanosensors can react with hydrogen atoms and detect any leak well before it would present a real threat, thus increasing the safety of the fuel cells.

Toyota has publicly stated it will introduce a fuel-cell car in Japan in 2003. Ford, Daimler-Chrysler, and Volkswagen are all also placing billion-dollar bets on fuel cells as the replacement for the internal-combustion engine. The bottom line is that the use of fuel cells will only increase as nanotechnology makes them more effective, and businesses, large and small, need to begin thinking about the transition today. Oil and gas executives will need to diversify their energy portfolios earlier, and owners of local gas stations will need to begin making plans to carry hydrogen a lot sooner than most ever expected (if they were expecting it at all).

As fuel cells find greater applications in cars, they will also find applications in businesses and homes. This is of major significance to every major energy company in the world as well as to any large user of electricity. With commercial buildings accounting for two-thirds of all electricity use in the United States, fuel cells will have a major impact on the profits of energy users and suppliers. It is likely that businesses will first begin employing fuel cells as a reliable secondary energy source (e.g., a single blackout as experienced in California in 2001 could cost a business millions of dollars), but as the price drops, people and businesses will begin to view them as a reasonable alternative to other energy sources—especially once the environmental benefits are factored into the equation. Energy companies—principally those that have long-term stranded costs (in the form of building nuclear or coal-burning plants or building and maintaining expensive support infrastructure like transmission lines)—need to begin understanding *today* how fuel cells will first erode and then eventually replace major components of their business.

MORE POWERFUL BATTERIES

Not all advances in nanotechnology between 2004–2005 will be so drastic. Batteries, a staple of modern life, fuel our cell phones, laptop computers, and watches, help our cars run, and power pacemakers, forklifts, and wheelchairs.

Carbon nanotubes, because of their atomic composition and shape, have the potential to store many more lithium ions than graphite, the material most commonly used today in rechargeable batteries. What this means is that your cell phone and laptops will go longer without recharging and be recharged faster. Imagine recharging your cell phone in less than a minute or using your laptop for ten straight hours. Thinner, more powerful batteries will also allow products to be redesigned, much the way superior technology allowed big, gray box computers to evolve into translucent, curved iMacs. By 2004, the technology will exist and have begun reaching the marketplace.

These advances will be of great convenience to the consumer and can dramatically affect the bottom line of companies involved in the $10 billion battery industry. For example, if existing batteries last longer, sales might decrease. Or if batteries can be recharged substantially more quickly, the market for disposable batteries may decrease because consumers won't be willing to pay when they can just recharge their existing battery in a couple of minutes or, possibly, seconds. Battery sales, on the other hand, also have the potential to increase if new applications suddenly become possible. Frequent travelers or consumers with small, crowded bathrooms might prefer to have smaller battery-operated hair dryers, curling irons, razors, and toothbrushes that can all be recharged by one simple device, thus reducing the nuisance of having multiple devices with electric cords.

Also, a variety of new and interesting applications might suddenly become possible as a result of longer-lasting batteries. For instance, toys might be able to perform new, more powerful functions, or electric cars might finally become practical because consumers won't have to recharge them every fifty miles or so.

CHEAPER NANOMATERIALS

From a minuscule $1.5 million in sales in 1999, the market for nanomaterials is estimated to grow to $430 million by the end of 2003. If it sustains an annual growth rate of 300 percent, the market will be $1.3 billion by 2004 and $5 billion by 2005.

These figures might prove to be conservative if the claim of Daniel Resasco, a chemical engineer at the University of Oklahoma, is true. Resasco reported in late 2001 that he had perfected a way to reduce the cost of single-walled carbon nanotubes from $500–$1,000 a gram to less than $6 a gram. Another company, Japan-based Frontier Carbon Corp., has reported that it expects to increase its carbon nanotube production from forty tons in 2003 to three hundred tons in 2004 and decrease its price to less than $4 per gram.

Presently carbon nanotubes are primarily being experimented with in universities and research labs around the world. By 2004, they will be employed in high-end applications by the military and NASA (where even slightly increased performance can justify large expenditures). At $4 to $6 a gram, however, a host of commercial opportunities become possible—everything from buildings and packaging products to super-lightweight golf clubs and bikes. Every company in the manufacturing sector will need to understand the capabilities of these new materials and recognize that there is likely a price point at which the materials they are using today are in jeopardy of being either enhanced with or replaced by new nanomaterials. Just as the advent of fiberglass decimated the entire wooden-boat-making industry after

World War II, cheap carbon nanotubes have the ability to do the same to many in the plastics, steel, aluminum, composite, and ceramics industries—especially when carbon nanotubes reach a price point similar to other bulk materials like polypropylene and iron ore.

The phenomenon of cheap nanomaterials is not, however, limited to carbon nanotubes. Nanostructured metals and alloys will regularly be applied along the joints of military aircraft to more than double their strength and failure resistance, and by 2004 most commercial aircraft companies will be planning to use nanostructured metals in their next generation of aircraft. Superior performance capabilities, reduced maintenance costs, and a significantly lower rate of stress failure are just some of the advantages the next generation of aircraft will possess because of nanotechnology.

The new nanomaterials, in addition to replacing the old products, might also open up new applications. For example, workers on assembly lines are required to wear bulky protective gear, but new stronger and lighter materials can be used to create slimmer uniforms, thereby increasing a company's profits by making their workers more nimble and thus more productive. The new nanomaterials can also help minimize injuries and thus benefit companies by saving time lost to accidents and reducing worker-compensation costs. Other uses might include: uniforms for prison guards, riot police, etc., more puncture-resistant scuba-diving suits, protective clothing for professional race-car drivers, and stronger and lighter shoulder pads for professional football players. How much is it worth to provide a star quarterback or running back, who earns $10-plus million a year, with equipment that will not only offer better protection, but yield an improvement in performance?

CATALYSTS AND FILTERS

More than one million diesel vehicles in California spew 28,000 tons of toxic particulates into the air every year. The particulates contribute to the state's severe smog problem, a problem that affects half the U.S. population according to the American Lung Association. A Johns Hopkins study has even estimated that nationwide dust and soot particles contribute to the premature deaths of between twenty and two hundred people a year.

Engelhard Corporation, located in New Jersey, is developing a diesel oxidation catalyst using nanoscale layers of platinum, palladium, and other precious metals to remove the toxic particles from the air. If this process is successful, smog alerts in major cities around the world may become a thing of the past. In fact, U.K.-based Oxonica planned to test a nanoparticle fuel additive in Hong Kong and six other Asian cities by late 2002. (Remember, researchers in Hong Kong are already experimenting with adding titanium dioxide nanoparticles to concrete as another method to address pollution.)

If state and federal governments suddenly begin requiring higher standards for particle matter (beginning in 2004, California will require 10 percent of all cars to be zero-emission vehicles), Engelhard and Oxonica are well positioned to help the automobile manufacturers meet the requirement. Conversely, the technology is also likely to result in governments passing new, tougher laws because regulators will want to push the emissions standards even higher.

Engelhard, however, is not just working on improving catalysts; they are also creating new nanofilters. For example, by 2004 it is likely they will have developed a product that can help oil companies clean up natural gas reserves that are contaminated by nitrogen (excess nitrogen reduces the heating capability of a gas). The filter, which has nano-sized pores that trap the nitrogen atoms, has the potential to reduce the amount of nitrogen in wells to the point where many of the contaminated gas reserves can become profitable. With an estimated 15 percent of wells falling into this category, the amount is not insubstantial in the oil and gas industry. The product may also prove to be a boon to consumers, who would benefit from lower prices in gas and oil as well as gas that burns more efficiently.

Improved nanofilters will also help the pharmaceutical industry make impurity-free drugs. Argonide Corporation, located in Stanford, Florida, has demonstrated that it can filter bacteria as small as 30 nanometers and achieve water purity of 99.99999 percent. Researchers at North Carolina State University have recently developed something called reverse selective membranes, which might further improve nanofilters to the point where they can be used for all types of purposes, including oil spills. These reverse selective membranes have the unusual property of catching smaller particles while allowing larger ones through. (Think of it this way: If the holes in a net are small enough to allow it to catch a ping-pong ball, it will also catch a baseball or basketball. Reverse selective membranes, however, can stop a ping-pong-sized molecule while allowing a basketball-sized molecule to go through.) It is this property that might theoretically allow a future nanofilter to catch tiny toxic molecules found in an oil spill while allowing the good molecules (for example, sea water and nutrients like plankton) to pass through. More immediate applications include helping natural gas suppliers and petroleum processors find a less energy-intensive and expensive method for separating gases.

COMMUNICATIONS

Picture a superhighway crowded with fast-moving cars. Now picture that superhighway coming to an abrupt stop at a river and all the cars stopping and getting on a slow ferry before they can restart their journey on the super-highway on the other side of the river.

Such a trip is analogous to what happens today in the world of fiber optics, where waves of light transmit data to a switching station. Because light diffuses over distance, it must be periodically reamplified at switching stations. The light is repackaged into electrical signals that a computer understands and can amplify or manipulate, and then it switches back to light and is forwarded to the next station.

Nano-sized lenses and filters, however, now have the ability to modulate and switch light, thus mitigating the cumbersome process of switching light into electrons and then back to light. The result is that the speed of optical networks will greatly increase, and the cost of transmitting vast amounts of data will decrease.

By 2004, the market for all-optical switches is expected to reach $1 billion. One company, NanoOpto, located in Somerset, New Jersey, is already producing devices for market. Companies making the older switching stations are at risk on two fronts. One, fewer stations will be required because the nano-sized lens can modulate the light better, meaning that longer distances between switching stations can be established. And two, the need for the equipment that converts the light into electrical signals and back will decrease.

The implications reach well beyond the $550 billion telecommunications industry to anyone who transmits data. If more data can be transferred more quickly and at a lower cost, what are the implications for long-distance health care? If a specialist in New York City can consult with a surgeon in a remote town in Canada in real time on a complicated procedure, what will that do to the health-care industry? What is the impact on the entertainment industry if not only promotional videos can be transmitted optically, but whole movies as well?

Tele-medicine and video-on-demand are already occurring, but what will be the impact on rural health-care centers and your local video-rental store if the technology continues driving the cost lower? How long will small health centers and large video chains be able to afford maintaining the physical infrastructure and staffing the workers required for their respective industries?

Everything from how we communicate (e.g., cheap video phones) to the nature of political campaigns to the education industry will be impacted as vast amounts of information and data can be cheaply transmitted in an engaging format. Consultants will also need to rethink how they offer services if the specifics of a complex problem can be transmitted optically. For example, if the problem can be addressed by issuing instructions optically, why pay for the expense of travel? And unlike the Internet, people will not need to be tied to their desktops. Problems can be viewed at the source, and instructions for solving the problem can be issued in real time.

Nanotech will also allow antennas to become more "adaptable," that is, they will be able to handle multiple transmissions. (Uniquely nanostructured materials that can open or close on demand will allow the antenna to receive and transmit over a large range of frequencies.) This means that your TV satellite system, Internet, cell phone, and even your home-security system can all use just one device. In addition to making the consumer's life easier, these devices will reduce the need for a number of communications receivers, transmitters, and antennas. Therefore, manufacturers of these devices need to be aware of this development.

Reconfigurable antennas and adjustable systems will pose a challenge for the FCC, the government agency that approves, regulates, and monitors spectrum use. It will need to adapt policies and metrics to accommodate spectrum modifications over the life of a communication system, whether earth- or space-based.

NEW EQUIPMENT AND NEW KNOWLEDGE

From 2004 through 2005, the U.S. government, working through the National Nanotechnology Initiative, has committed to developing better measuring and modeling equipment. Everything from a better understanding of the chemical, electrical, and magnetic properties of atoms to more sophisticated modeling will result. The impact of understanding how atoms work and interact will undoubtedly create new and exciting developments in the field and set the stage for the next round of nanotechnology development.

NANOPOINTS

* Does any portion of your business rely on treating specific diseases? If so, what is the impact on your business if a new drug addresses the disease?

* How will your insurance premiums change if nanotechnology either eliminates some diseases or, alternatively, requires that insurance cover a host of new diseases that can now be treated?

* Can nanosensors be employed in any aspect of your business? For example, is your product temperature- or humidity-sensitive?

* Do you need a reliable secondary energy source? Can fuel cells be utilized by your business?

* Does your company supply the automotive industry? If fuel cells begin gradually replacing the internal-combustion engine, does your product lose out?

* Can any of your products be redesigned or new applications conceived if batteries become thinner and more powerful?

* Will your manufacturing process need to be modified as new nanomaterials are introduced?

* Is there a price point at which either carbon nanotubes or certain nanoparticles can be utilized profitably in your business? Is someone in your company researching this information?

* What aspects of your business will change if data and information can be transmitted faster, cheaper, and more clearly?

CHAPTER SIX

2006-2008: The Avalanche Begins

"IT'S HARD TO THINK OF AN INDUSTRY THAT ISN'T
GOING TO BE DISRUPTED BY NANOTECHNOLOGY."

—DAVID BISHOP, DIRECTOR OF MEMS RESEARCH,
LUCENT TECHNOLOGIES

On October 15, 2001, Bethlehem Steel declared bankruptcy. In spite of being one of the original thirty companies listed on the Dow Jones Industrial Average, in spite
of producing most of the steel for the U.S. warships in
World War II, in spite of having invested billions of dollars in technology, and in spite of being named one of the
best-managed companies in the U.S. as late as 1989,
Bethlehem could not compete with nimbler, smaller, and
more efficient minimills that found a better and cheaper
way to produce superior steel. And in a move that is as
symbolic as it is ironic, the vast machine shop of the
Bethlehem Steel plant is now slated to become home to
the National Museum of Industrial History. Some will
argue that Bethlehem and the other twenty-seven U.S.

steel companies that have filed for bankruptcy since 1998 were victims of unscrupulous foreign competitors that illegally dumped cheap steel on the U.S. market. The stark truth is that they were not competitive.

No industry is safe from the powerful forces of technological innovation—a lesson that the $139 billion semiconductor industry would be wise to take to heart *now*. It is a sobering thought that global leaders in the industry could be relegated to the ash heap of history by advances in nanotechnology—but it is possible. (Executives at Bethlehem in 1989 would likely have scoffed at the notion that they would be bankrupt in twelve years and that their main facility would be transformed into a museum.)

Among the industries and businesses that can expect to see their economic landscape transformed during the period of 2006 to 2008 are the publishing, advertising, food, and clothing industries. It is, however, the semiconductor industry and in particular the silicon computer chip—the foundation of the modern Information Age—that will first feel the pressure. The pressure will be applied from three separate directions, and nanotechnology will be involved in all three: super chips, plastic semiconductors, and carbon nanotubes.

SILICON SUCCESS AND A BRICK WALL

For four decades, silicon has served as the material of choice for the information era. There are many reasons for its success—namely, it is abundant, effective, and can be mass produced—but time is potentially running out for silicon. Moore's First Law, which stipulates that the computing power of silicon chips doubles every eighteen months, is expected to run up against the laws of physics in ten years. One of the reasons is that as transistors get ever-smaller, unwanted leakage current begins to bleed through the thin insulation layers of the transistors and wreaks havoc on the performance of the chip. Second, as semiconductors become more integrated with a greater number of transistors, more power is required to operate the transistors, which translates into more heat. (For comparative purposes, today's Pentium IV has 42 million transistors, but Intel expects its next generation Itanium processor to have 220 million transistors.) Dealing with the excessive heat these transistors create is a serious problem that may no longer be able to be addressed by cooling fans in the computer. The third problem is that as the transistors get smaller, the fabrication facilities used to design and manufacture these chips become more sophisticated and more costly to build. Within ten years, industry experts estimate that the cost of these facilities will range between $10 and $50 billion. If true, few companies will be able to remain competitive in such a capital-intensive industry.

SUPER CHIPS

Silicon will not, however, be easily replaced. Chip manufacturers are comfortable with the material, and their entire multibillion-dollar infrastructure is set up to deal with it. (Radical change is never easy, even for an industry as dynamic as the semiconductor industry.) But this is precisely why nanotechnology will be implemented, because it will allow chipmakers to add new materials to silicon to enhance its performance without having to redesign or otherwise change their manufacturing processes. For example, nanotechnology will enable silicon and gallium arsenide (which are structurally incompatible) to operate in the same device by adding a nanolayer of compatible material between them. This is a huge advantage. Gallium arsenide can handle wireless communications and transmit light, allowing such a chip to perform new functions and operate at higher speeds. It is why these hybrid chips are referred to as "super chips."

While this development is extremely important to the semiconductor industry because it represents a qualitative improvement in its products' performance, the impact of these super chips will be even greater on the businesses that use them. For example, gallium arsenide will make for more powerful cell phones, gallium nitride will be used to enhance memory storage, and indium phosphide will allow optical networks to perform at extremely high levels and over long distances. Motorola is already working with gallium arsenide, and it is likely that by 2006 it will have developed a series of chips with novel performance capabilities that are price competitive with plain silicon. Applications, in the short term, will range from a "smart" phone that will be able to tell you where the closest grocery store is to longer-range applications such as an Internet-enabled cereal box that could serve up the morning news or an e-mail from your daughter along with your cereal. Cheap computer chips with wireless capability are what will make this possible.

These super chips will allow product designers to add wireless communication devices to a variety of products that have never before been equipped with such abilities. For example, your refrigerator will be able to monitor energy prices via the Internet and connect to the energy grid only when prices are off-peak or, alternatively, only when the refrigerator absolutely needs energy to maintain a certain temperature. This means that both businesses and individuals can better control their energy costs, while energy companies themselves may find overall demand for their product going down due to the increased efficiency that these super chips provide. Smart chips embedded in car tires will tell your car when the tires need air or have to be rotated, suggesting that fewer tires will be sold because consumers will keep their tires in optimum condition. Furthermore, these super chips, if embedded in products, will allow businesses to maintain excellent control over their inventory. They will be able to know everything about a product from the time it is produced to the time it is sold.

PLASTIC SEMICONDUCTORS

As potentially important as these super chips are, they pale in comparison to a more significant development that will begin making its presence felt between 2006 and 2008: plastic semiconductors. Manufactured by regular inkjet printers spraying out superfine, precise nanoparticles onto a thin film, these circuits can be bonded to rigid and flexible materials. Plastic Logic, based in Cambridge, England, and FLEXIC, located in Milpitas, California, are already working on developing prototype materials based on this technology. No longer will semiconductor applications be limited by the constraints of silicon, which is fairly rigid and thus limits how and where it can be used. Unlike silicon semiconductors, plastic ones do not need to be made in expensive clean rooms, nor are they made using toxic etching chemicals. This means they can be cheaply produced, and they have the added benefit of being able to print in low quantities for special projects. The transistors fabricated by this process are much larger than today's silicon transistors and will not replace super computer chips for high-end applications or dense memories. However, the ability to make electronic circuits cheaply and on a flexible material will open many niche markets not available to traditional silicon technology.

What this technology implies is that the manufacturing process that today's chipmakers are using may soon find competition from a printed technology. If powerful, flexible, and multifaceted circuits can be inexpensively printed out like sheets of wallpaper, at room temperature, in plants that don't have to be superclean, then the very nature of the semiconductor industry will be changed. A company will not need the massive infrastructure— specifically the multibillion-dollar fabrication plants—to produce semiconductor devices.

But like the super chips before it, plastic semiconductors will have their largest "disruptive" potential on end users. The fact that these chips will be thin, light, flexible, and capable of dynamically changing color pixels means that "electronic paper" is right around the corner and will become available during this period.

The implications are astounding. By connecting to a wireless adapter, electronic paper will be able to access the Internet and change the image being shown on the paper. As the technology progresses and as users become more comfortable with it, electronic paper is going to require the $60 billion newspaper, the $59 billion periodical, and the $23 billion book publishing industries to rethink their business models. There is no reason why customers won't be able to tailor their morning newspaper to their specific tastes. For example, an individual might prefer to read the sports section from the *Boston Globe,* the marketing section from *The Wall Street Journal,* the technology section from Wired.com, national politics from *The Washington Post,* foreign affairs from *The London Times* and *Japan Times,* and the latest in nano-technology from smalltimes.com. And rather than having to purchase five separate papers and visit two separate websites, the person can download all the relevant articles directly to his thin, flexible electronic paper. And unlike viewing articles from the Internet today, the person will be able to hold the "paper," which may even have the texture of real paper, and take it with him anywhere. The electronic paper is also likely to be easy on the eye (unlike today's computer screens) because carbon nanotubes— such as those that will be used in flat panel displays by late 2003—will ensure that the pixels are bright, vivid, and viewable under any condition. Unlike e-books, which have never really caught on with the consumer, electronic paper will not require the consumer to adjust behavior substantially. For example, electronic paper can be modi-fied to fit the size, feel, and look of a newspaper. Furthermore, because it will be flexible, lightweight, and have fast download speeds and low power requirements, the electronic paper will be much more convenient than e-books. (Even with these advantages, people might still prefer regular books for the simple reasons that they enjoy the sensation of flipping a page or because they like to display the books they have read in their bookcases.)

This technology will not only impact the publishing world, it will disrupt the $108 billion U.S. printing indus-try. Books and papers will still be published, but as consumers such as schools and universities come to understand that textbooks can be updated almost instantly, printing and shipping a wide variety of new textbooks every year will seem like an extravagant waste. (Note: Nanotechnology, because it will enable faster computers, may advance the raw pace of new knowledge in the fields of physics, chemistry, and biology so fast that paper textbooks might no longer be practical because things are changing so quickly.) Amazon.com, Federal Express, and United Parcel Service may feel a slight impact as fewer hard-copy publications are ordered and shipped.

While such changes might cause these industries concern, the flip side is that new markets might potentially open. For example, people who did not previously read the newspaper or buy books might be more inclined to do so if they knew that much of the information could be transmitted visually on the printed page. (Just imagine, for instance, if you could not only read about last night's thrilling NBA overtime victory but could also view the winning basket.) And the demand for content-providers, such as writers and video-production specialists, might increase as the demand for information increases.

Books and paper are not, however, the only industries to be impacted by the advances that plastic semiconductors will enable. By 2006, the use of electronic billboards (nanostructured thin films) will be eroding a sizable share of the market for in-store displays and billboards. These thin films, which are only a few atoms thick and will be controlled with plastic semiconductors, can change color under the appropriate electrical influence. NTera, a company based in Dublin, Ireland, is already working on this technology. What this means is that in-store displays, such as those showing prices, can change instantly. The development is not insignificant when one considers that a retailer like Macy's spends $250,000 a week just to change signs in its stores.

The ramifications for the $85 billion advertising industry are also huge. Imagine the impact on the advertising industry if instead of sending out crews of workers to change billboards every few weeks, the signs could be changed instantly from the comfort of the home office. Not only will advertisers be able to change signs on demand and cheaply, they can better target audiences for their customers. For example, the people going into downtown Chicago at eight in the morning are far different from those going into the city at eight in the evening. An advertiser might be able to sell the space to Starbucks in the morning, the Chicago Cubs in the afternoon (alerting people that tickets for the afternoon game are still available), and Budweiser in the evening. Depending on the market, the pricing structure of new billboards can also change to reflect the audience they want to reach.

SUPER CHIPS + PLASTIC SEMICONDUCTORS

The combination of super chips with plastic semiconductors will take the level of disruption one step further. If high-performance super chips can be embedded in certain high-end products like kitchen appliances and cheap, flexible chips made from plastic can be incorporated into packaging, this means that a milk carton in your refrigerator will be able to communicate with your home computer to tell you that it is time to order more milk, and your dinner container will tell the microwave when it is fully cooked. Cars will soon be able to "talk" with their outside environment because the chips, in addition to having processing, memory, and global positioning system

(GPS) capability, will also contain radio-frequency devices. This means that a computer in your car could theoretically query every restaurant in a two-mile radius to learn what the daily specials are and if a table is available for lunch.

Singapore is already requiring cars to be embedded with smart chips so that government officials can "price" road usage. The hope is that by sending the appropriate market signals (e.g., charging higher prices when the roads are most congested), consumers will modify their driving habits and traffic congestion will be eased because some people will seek to minimize their costs, preferring instead to do their driving when the roads are not so expensive. And while Singapore is already using this technology, the point is that by 2006 the power and the price of these chips will have reached such a level that super chips and plastic semiconductors will start popping up everywhere. Then not only will Singapore price road usage, it will be able to direct and manage traffic in real time because the cheap plastic chips will be embedded everywhere from buildings to lampposts. (Note: Simply because one country, such as Singapore, which has a history of strong governmental action, adopts a technology does not mean it will be adopted everywhere. In fact, privacy advocates and those who fear excessive government control will likely oppose such a technology strongly.)

The list of possible applications is, however, almost limitless. If efficient markets are dictated by good information, then by the middle of this decade, the market will have ratcheted itself up to a new level of efficiency because of the new applications, the power, and the ubiquitous nature of these devices. Their influence will only continue to grow in the years ahead.

CARBON NANOTUBES AND NANOWIRES

The third computer-related nanotechnology development during this period will be the use of solid nanowires or ultrathin nanotubes (1.4 nanometers wide) in conjunction with silicon transistors. These nanotubes may be fabricated using carbon, gallium arsenide, or a variety of other semiconducting materials. Computers made from these materials will initially be very expensive and will be developed for niche applications. But because they will be smaller, require less energy, and be substantially more powerful—perhaps by as much as a factor of 10 to 100 over today's computers—they will lead to a bounty of new applications.

Because of the increased computing power, longer-term weather forecasting will become more accurate through more sophisticated modeling and pattern recognition and will offer earlier warnings of weather-related natural disasters like hurricanes and blizzards. Citizens and insurance companies alike will benefit as they are able to take more precautionary actions and reduce the amount of damage Mother Nature inflicts. Other businesses, such as those whose profits rely on travel (e.g., the airlines and trucking industries), will be able to better adjust their schedules to minimize the delays and costs associated with weather problems. Other industries, like agriculture, will be able to optimize resources by working with Mother Nature—for example, by conserving water if rain is imminent.

This new modeling can also be applied to address larger problems. Very complex organizations, like the ecosystem, could be modeled to gain a better understanding of how different environmental factors affect various species and habitats. For instance, ecologists could study how global warming affects everything from the milk production of cows to the mating habits of insects. How these subtle changes ripple across the environment can also be better understood (e.g., if a certain insect population decreases due to global warming, what will be the impact on the entire food chain?).

More powerful computers will also begin to understand and interpret text and drawings and draw rational inferences from the information. Many jobs, particularly those in which a shortage of workers exists today and in which some of the tasks are very tedious or time-consuming (e.g., qualified patent attorneys) will be delegated to computers. For example, it will make little sense for lawyers, who are billing out at a rate of $200 an hour, to search patent databases or real estate deeds when a computer can do a portion of the job.

Countless other businesses will be able to employ these computers to search large databases to uncover trends and identify societal impacts that are currently missed or ignored. And businesses that are already employing powerful computers to design and test prototypes of products before the actual physical products are made will be able to do even more with these nanotechnology-enabled computers.

The implications of the kind of power we are describing are hard to fathom because vast amounts of seemingly worthless data, if pieced together with other mundane information, might yield significant developments. For example, if smart chips become ubiquitous and computers powerful enough, there is no reason why hundreds of factors such as weather and passenger and gate information could not be safely and accurately calculated to allow aircraft to land and take off whenever they were ready. Think of it this way: Why should man, with all this computing power, be required to line up methodically on the tarmac and wait to be told when it is safe to take off, when a flock of a thousand birds can scatter on a moment's notice without even one bird bumping into another?

"BOUTIQUE" MATERIALS

As a result of the better understanding of the chemical, electrical, structural, optical, and magnetic properties of atoms that will be enabled by previous nanotech developments, scientists and researchers will also be able to employ these new computers to model, predict, design, and build entirely new materials. This will be a qualitative improvement over many of the materials mentioned in the previous chapter. Whereas those advances were about improving *existing* materials by adding carbon nanotubes or unique nanoparticles, material science during this period will advance to the point where entirely new materials can be created with precise specifications. Up to this point in history, mankind has simply reshaped the materials Mother Nature has provided us. Humans will now be able to take the next step and create materials that even Mother Nature has not been able to fashion in her 3.8 billion years.

The Defense Department is working to create materials for its jet fighters that are not only stronger and lighter, but also radar- and sound-absorbing and self-repairing. These properties will allow fighters and other military aircraft to make longer missions and reach their destination faster with less chance of detection. The U.S. Navy is attempting to construct new paints that mimic the skin of a shark to allow their submarines to slice through the water more efficiently. The development of these new materials will eventually affect everyone from automobile and ship manufacturers to structural engineers, who will be able to design new buildings and new products. Even the windshield-repair businesses will be affected because certain molecules will be made to reconfigure themselves when heat is applied to them, thus creating continuously self-repairing plastic windshields.

New nanomaterials might even cause society to move back in time, in a sense. Stronger, lighter, and safer materials might make blimp cargo lifters a viable option for some transportation needs. By 2006, it is estimated that blimps will be capable of carrying more than 160 tons, meaning these massive vehicles might populate the skies over Atlanta as they carry freight over congested highways en route to regional distribution centers in Miami, Memphis, and Raleigh. Depending on traffic conditions and the cost of fuel around many of the country's urban centers, it is possible that Federal Express, UPS, and the U.S. Postal Service will employ some number of these blimps to deliver bulky or low-priority cargo efficiently to regional distribution nodes.

New nanomaterials might also facilitate the creation of super-lightweight, solar-power gliders that never have to land. These vehicles can serve as communication hubs, supplementing satellite-communication networks over densely populated or remote areas.

Nanomaterials will also continue to reduce both the weight of spacecraft and the size of products that are transported into space. One immediate application is that satellites will continue to be made lighter and the cost per satellite of launching them into space will continue to decrease. The implication is that any product or process that employs satellite or GPS technology will benefit. Farmers can receive real-time, accurate weather information, and shipping companies can track their shipments with precision and issue directions to their drivers based on real-time driving conditions. While much of this technology already exists, the point is that by 2006 to 2008 the power of the technology will have increased exponentially while simultaneously experiencing a sharp reduction in price. The difference will be a qualitative improvement in performance. For example, whereas today's GPS technology can tell a driver to avoid a certain road during rush hour, tomorrow's technology will be able to tell the driver in real time which streets and roads to take in order to minimize driving time.

And while some new nanomaterials will take us back to the past, the preponderance of these new materials will propel us into the future at breakneck speed. In 2002, MIT received a $50 million grant to create the new Institute for Soldier Nanotechnologies, a center designed to develop materials and devices for the soldier of the future. Private industry, including DuPont, Raytheon, and Massachusetts General Hospital, is contributing an additional $40 million to augment the institute.

The center, from which the Army expects to spin off commercial applications, will focus on threat-detection (E. coli sensors), real-time automated medical treatment, threat-neutralization (slimmer bulletproof clothing, etc.), concealment (clothes that change color or make the wearer nearly invisible), reduced logistical footprints (making equipment lighter), and enhanced human performance (soldiers capable of jumping six to twenty feet in the air). This last capability, it is thought, will be enabled by nanoscopic molecules that are housed in the base of a soldier's boot and deflate like an accordion in their natural state but rapidly expand when electricity is applied. Once the current (which the soldier will control) ceases, the molecule shrinks to its natural shape and awaits the next jolt.

The commercial potential of these nanotechnologies is astounding. Supersensitive detection systems will be employed above the entrances of hospitals to detect whether visitors are carrying pathogens that might harm patients. Lightweight, bulletproof clothing might find markets among business executives who fear attack (but don't want to appear to have heavy protection) as well as people in high-risk neighborhoods.

Clothing that can detect and render harmless deadly toxins for a soldier is likely to find applications in counteracting harmful bacteria and eventually maybe even viruses in the civilian population. For example, doctors and nurses might wear scrubs embedded with antibacterial agents, and the parents of young children, especially those in day care or school where airborne illnesses seem to travel with amazing speed, may choose to outfit their children with clothing that can kill the common cold virus.

If the Army can devise and manufacture clothing that can change color, adjust for temperature, and monitor the wearer's vital signs, as is expected, what are the implications for fashion designers? At a minimum, they will need to rethink the age-old question of form versus function. For example, will consumers be willing to have a jacket for every season of the year if new nanomaterials can be embedded in fabric to accommodate outside conditions? And if consumers are not buying as many items of clothing because they can change color or can be used in multiple seasons, what will be the impact of the $181 billion apparel industry? More subtle implications might include the impact on suitcase manufacturers as travelers pack fewer clothes. (Note: Making clothes change color on demand relies on the techniques of chameleons and squids, which can adapt to the colors in their environment almost instantly. Nanotechnology mimics the animal methods by modifying the size and shapes of nanocrystals through electrical current. Depending on their size and shape, the color will change accordingly. Researchers at DuPont are, in fact, working on this technology today.)

The institute is also committed to reducing a soldier's equipment load by fifty pounds or more. If successful, the implications will extend well beyond the 376,000 firefighters around the country, for whom wearing lighter gear and carrying lighter equipment into a blazing fire may be the difference between life and death, to any application such as portable medical kits or camping products where the weight of the product can be reduced without sacrificing performance.

These as well as other nanomaterials will also find a place in large-scale construction materials. Bridges will be able to expand and contract with temperature changes without cracking or deteriorating. Buildings will be better able to withstand high winds and earthquakes. And a variety of other structures and products can be made cleaner, safer, and more efficient. For example, building exteriors may change color to reflect heat in the summer, or automotive radiators can be designed with new materials that allow eighteen-wheelers to be modified into more sleek, aerodynamic (and thus fuel-efficient) vehicles. (Currently radiators, which resemble big blocks, act like huge parachutes and require the trucks to unnecessarily push air down the road.)

DRUGS AND DIET

One of the more likely nanotechnology scenarios to play out during this period will be the advent of "portable pharmacies." These pharmacies are not the brick-and-mortar variety that most of us visit to get a prescription filled. Rather, they are small, implantable micro-sized devices that will carry dozens of drugs, in the form of nanoparticles, that can be electronically dispensed at regular intervals over long periods. (The FDA could possibly delay the introduction of a variety of nanoparticles until they can be determined to not have an adverse affect on people.)

Elderly patients, many of whom take anywhere from two to forty different drugs a day, can be relieved of the time-consuming and confusing process of taking different drugs at different times. Similarly, other patients, for example Alzheimer's or mentally ill patients (or their caregivers), who often have trouble remembering when and which drug to administer, can be relieved of this burden. The implication for pharmacies and the more than 200,000 pharmacists is that their workload and job function will change greatly as a result of these new technologies.

Another industry that is likely to feel the affect of nanotechnology is the $40 billion diet industry. Government researchers are currently working on creating nanoparticle taste-enhancers (unique molecules that can enhance a particular taste) that can be added to low-calorie foods to increase the richness of flavor. These taste-enhancers are likely to be ready for the market between 2006 and 2008. Just imagine what a low-calorie chocolate Hershey bar, one that tastes exactly like its high-calorie cousin but with none of the low-cal aftertaste, will do to the $13 billion chocolate market. Further, if more people are eating more chocolate without guilt, what will they be eating *less* of?

Along these same lines, the $42 billion diet-supplement market is likely to be shaken up in this period. An Israeli company, Nutralease, is working on developing nanoparticles that deliver nutraceuticals (organic health-care ingredients) to produce better health results. The nanoparticles are tailored to protect the molecules of the nutraceuticals until they can be safely delivered to their destination, e.g., the heart or the colon, depending on what ailment is being addressed. For example, phytosterol, a product derived from soy oil, has proven successful in reducing cholesterol in patients by 15 percent over a four-week period. Currently the product is added to margarine, meaning that those who want to benefit from it must eat the margarine. Nutralease, however, is planning on delivering phytosterol directly to the patient either in the form of a pill or, perhaps, even by adding it to a drink. If successful, the sales of the cholesterol-reducing drug Lipitor, America's leading cholesterol-lowering prescription drug, may plummet. Nutralease is also working on developing a nanoparticle to carry lycopene, the red pigment from tomatoes, which has been demonstrated to reduce the risk of breast and prostate cancer. If successful, people who are diagnosed with a greater risk to develop these cancers (which is likely to be possible due to the nanotechnology-related developments in disease detection discussed in the previous chapter) will be able to take preventative action by simply consuming a drink that contains the nanoparticles.

By 2006, chances are that Nutralease's nanoparticles will have received government approval to be used on humans. If so, the entire diet-supplement market had better be prepared. If people can take smaller but more effective doses of natural ingredients without resorting to eating unwanted products or less-than-tasteful products, a significant portion of the diet-supplement market will be disrupted.

ENVIRONMENTAL CLEANUP

Over the next thirty years, the U.S. government is expected to spend $750 billion on cleaning up contaminated environmental sites. Nanoparticles, however, have the potential to reduce this amount substantially by reacting with and neutralizing harmful chemical agents. For example, nanoparticles consisting of 99.9 percent iron and .1 percent palladium have been pumped into groundwater to decontaminate both the water and soil of carcinogenic solvents (of the variety used in the dry-cleaning industry, for example).

One company, Trane, based in New Jersey, has tested nanoparticles in sample wells and found they have been able to reduce toxic chemicals in water by as much as 96 percent. The previous best that the company was able to achieve was a 25 percent reduction. These nanoparticles, if they receive regulatory approval, will improve the availability and supply of clean water and reduce the need for expensive water-treatment and -purification plants (and the power to run them). This will have a global impact, especially in developing nations where many diseases are transmitted through the water supply and where the cost of cleaning water is high.

New nanoparticles might hold the answer to neutralizing the runoff from pesticides and other agricultural chemicals, with the impact again being global in nature. Consider that agricultural pesticides found in the Gulf of Mexico, where they have created a massive "dead zone" in which no fish can survive, have been traced all the way back up the Mississippi River to Minnesota farms. This suggests that these nanoparticles might not only help make the Mississippi River clean for young kids to swim in, but that Louisiana shrimpers might eventually be able to return closer to shore.

Researchers at Lehigh University have also successfully tested nanoparticles to detoxify cyanide, suggesting that other nanoparticles might work in a similar fashion against other deadly chemicals and agents. In addition to making water safer, nanoparticles might be able to *keep* it that way; this technology may eliminate the ability of bioterrorists to contaminate the water supply.

The technology can also reduce the cost of remediating environmental cleanup sites. In addition to sparing companies significant cleanup expenses, legal expenses can be reduced as the health-care liabilities associated with these sites (as documented in the books and movies *Erin Brockovich* and *A Civil Action*) can be mitigated. Any business or municipality that is dealing with groundwater or environmental cleanup issues or is considering developing land on an old industrial site needs to be aware of this technology because it has the potential to return a lot of land to productive use.

It has even been speculated that three-dimensional nanomaterials can be manufactured to encapsulate the radioactive ions from nuclear waste. These nanomaterials could individually enclose the radioactive substance in a defect-free material, reducing the potential for cracking and leakage. In fact, to ensure safety, multilayers of nano-materials could be used. The materials could even have special radiation properties as well as sensors and wireless-transmission capabilities to monitor status constantly. If so, the ramifications for the energy industry might be huge—especially if the thorny issue of storing nuclear waste can be satisfactorily addressed. Opponents of the U.S. government's plan to store nuclear waste in the Yucca Mountains in Nevada might have an additional argument in their favor if such a technology pans out. Why risk shipping toxic and lethal material across the country on trains and by truck when a safer alternative might be available through nano-technology?

As futuristic and as fantastic as some of these developments sound, the technology for each is being developed now. The fact that they are only three to five years away from the marketplace means that they must be incorporated into your long-range planning today.

NANOPOINTS

- ✳ Are there applications for super chips in your product? Can product performance be enhanced? Can new applications be developed?
- ✳ If electronics become flexible, can your product be redesigned? Are new applications possible?
- ✳ Can your inventory be better managed through cheap, flexible chips? Can they be embedded in more products to provide better tracking information?
- ✳ Are there aspects of your business (or your job) that can now be done by more powerful computers? What are the potential savings?

* Can more powerful computers and more sophisticated software help your company better plan for the future by running multiple "what-if" scenarios over different time-frames (one, two, five, or ten years)? And will your scenario modeling need to utilize a wider set of assumptions to account for new nanotechnology-related developments?
* What are the implications to your business if your chief competitor is using more sophisticated modeling software and cuts in half both the cost of production and the time-to-market?
* Can nanotechnology-enabled advances be employed to deliver advertising messages to your target audience more effectively?
* Will nanoparticle taste-enhancers or nutraceuticals affect any portion of your business?
* How may your health or insurance benefits be changed by nanotechnology diagnostics?
* Does your business supply or rely on retail clothing sales? If so, how might new nanomaterials impact your bottom line?
* Can you employ more environmentally friendly nano-materials or nanoparticles to reduce environmental costs while simultaneously making yourself more attractive to investors?

CHAPTER SEVEN

2009-2013: Taking Control

"NANOSTRUCTURING REPRESENTS THE BEGINNING
OF A REVOLUTIONARY NEW AGE IN OUR ABILITY TO
MANIPULATE MATERIALS FOR THE GOOD OF
HUMANITY."

—WORLD TECHNOLOGY EVALUATION CENTER
PANEL REPORT ON NANOSTRUCTURED
SCIENCE AND TECHNOLOGY

Imagine a mechanic at the end of the nineteenth century being presented with a broken-down automobile manufactured in the late twentieth century. If he looked under the hood, he might have been able to grasp the concept behind the working of the internal-combustion engine. He might even have been able to make some crude repairs to get the car operating. His ability to repair the automobile totally, however, would be hindered by an incomplete understanding of the machine and its sophisticated tool requirements.

This analogy is comparable to what today's medical professionals know about the human body. They can understand how the body works in a general sense, and they can even repair it in many instances. Their understanding of how the body works at the nanoscale, however, where complex molecular interactions govern, is limited. Furthermore, they lack many of the tools needed to repair the body at this nanoscale level. This means many medical operations are, at best, limited in scope and, at worst, crude, temporary, and ineffective measures (e.g., chemotherapy) that do little more than postpone the inevitable.

Near the end of the decade, by 2009, this equation will change. Our understanding of how the human body really works will accelerate because the processes will be observed in real time with powerful new nanotechnology tools. Medical professionals will constantly add to their knowledge and thus develop ever-more-effective methods for treating and preventing disease. Also, by this time, many of the medical applications of nanotechnology that were only in laboratories or were in various clinical stages of FDA approval earlier in the decade will be in public use. For example, convenient treatments (and possibly even cures) for AIDS, diabetes, sexually transmitted diseases, and a number of different cancers will be on the market.

A number of other ailments will also likely be addressed as the intricacies of each disease's progression and the secrets to stopping it are revealed by nanotechnology. Muscular dystrophy, a disease that, according to the NIH, affects 250,000 people in the United States, results in muscles being gradually replaced by scar tissue and fat. Sufferers of this disease are missing the molecule dystrophin. If a drug platform can be found to deliver and attach the molecule where it is needed, a cure for the debilitating disease is possible.

Much more prevalent medical problems will also

benefit from nanotech. According to the NIH, twenty-two percent of Americans are obese (defined as a Body Mass Index of 25 or greater, where the BMI is calculated using age, height, and weight). It is a disease that erodes the quality of life for millions of people, and it is rising in epidemic portions among the country's youth. The medical costs are also rising. A significant portion of the $286 billion cost of cardiovascular disease in the U.S. can be attributed to obesity. Researchers in Canada believe an enzyme called protein tyrosine phosphatase may hold a clue to treating the disease. In a study with rats, the researchers have found that those injected with the enzyme can eat a high-fat diet without gaining much weight. A number of people and businesses associated with treating obesity—including Weight Watchers, Jenny Craig, the makers of "lite" food and diet soda, publishers of fitness and diet magazines, and health-club operators—will all be impacted.

Parkinson's, Huntington's, schizophrenia, and a host of other diseases are believed to be genetic, so a similar molecular (e.g. nanotech) solution might work. Food intolerances of every variety, from milk and eggs to chocolate, may be alleviated because the enzymes that digest these substances can be reproduced in individuals who lack them. Information yielded through nanotechnology-enabled advances offers possible solutions to these ailments within the decade.

Even drug abuse and addiction, which cost the U.S. economy more than $110 billion annually, may find a remedy in nanotech. Genetic factors are widely believed to make people more or less susceptible to addiction. In one study, people with a gene variant in the enzyme CYP2A6 were found to metabolize nicotine more slowly.

The study found that these people were also less likely to become addicted. If nanotechnology can replicate the enzyme, the implications for the $165 billion tobacco industry are staggering—not to mention the potential savings in health care if the number of smokers significantly decreases. The market for tobacco products would diminish as those smokers who couldn't overcome the hurdle of addiction would now be able to.

It's not only research with enzymes that will be big news at the end of the decade. James Baker, a leading researcher in the field of nanobiotechnology at the University of Michigan, is making great progress in developing unique nanoscale dendrimers, which are synthetically manufactured devices. These tree-branch-shaped devices, which are created nanometer by nanometer, can be manufactured with almost any number of branches (which are necessary to hold different molecules and nanoparticles) and are small enough to fit inside a human cell.

One of the most promising applications calls for using a dendrimer to carry different chemical tools to locate, tag, kill, and remove a cancer cell. Imagine the dendrimer as a highly trained military commando team. One chemical, specifically modified to bind itself to a target, will help the device "land" on the right spot. A second chemical will "tag" the cancer cell and tell your doctor where the cancer is located. Think of it as someone shooting a flare. A third chemical will act as the assassin and kill the cancer cell. A fourth agent will act as a radioman and send a signal that the cancer cell has been eliminated, and the fifth chemical, acting as an evacuation squad, will flush the dead cell out of the body.

The implications of such a device are astounding. A single device—one smaller than a human cell—has the potential to alter radically how cancer is treated and, in the process, disrupt the work of a variety of different medical professionals and eliminate significant segments of the medical market. For example, if cancer cells can be identified and eliminated early, the need for a large number of highly specialized oncologists will decrease. If chemotherapy and radiation are no longer required, the number of specialists in these fields will decrease, and the companies that supply the equipment will see their business erode, as will much of the work and business that goes into caring for and helping cancer survivors recover from treatment.

Not only will patients with a disease be helped by nanotechnology, but those with physical limitations such as blindness or hearing loss will also be aided. Using nanotechnology, parts of our bodies that already operate at the nanoscale, such as the retinal cones and rods that allow sight and the stereocilia in the inner ear that allow hearing, can be replicated. When these ultraresponsive nanostructures are placed on nanometer-thin ceramics or other biologically compatible material, they can be embedded in the body to provide sight and hearing.

Near the end of the decade, information obtained from uncoding the human genome, proteome, and other molecular interactions, along with a better understanding of how molecules interact and more powerful computers to model, design, test, and produce new drugs, will revolutionize health care. Not only will the amount of medical information explode within the decade, but patients will become more knowledgeable as they obtain more information about their health condition at a much earlier stage. The pendulum of care will continue to swing in favor of the patient as early diagnosis and prevention take precedence over treatment.

The nanotechnology-enabled advance that will most affect this paradigm shift will be the easy, cheap, and rapid deployment of nanosensors to detect the early onset of diseases. For example, testing for strep, bronchitis, or pneumonia at home using a simple plastic stick in your mouth will be possible. Why go to a doctor's office when an inexpensive and accurate diagnostic system can provide the same information quickly and in the privacy of your own home?

SENSORS

Throughout the twentieth century, cancer was misdiagnosed or missed altogether at an average rate of 40 percent. By 2009, the DNA- and protein-based systems (discussed in chapter four) that are able to conduct tests for thousands of diseases on the spot, with redundancies built in to ensure accuracy, will now be available in home-based systems. Using tiny nanoprobes that can be painlessly inserted into an arm to test the blood or by using nanosensors embedded in a toothbrush, individuals can test for illnesses on a daily basis. Earlier detection will lead to earlier treatment, which will produce far better results at a fraction of the cost. Just as the dentistry industry has changed its focus over the years from emergency treatment toward preventative and personalized treatment, so will health care.

Nanosensors will not be limited to just the medical arena. Within the decade, *anything* that has value will have its own sensor and be embedded with a unique identification code and supported by a plastic semiconductor computer and a wireless communication capability. The owner will be able to locate it on command and communicate with it if necessary. Because products will be able to be located instantly, they will be more difficult to lose; and because the sensors will allow them to be programmed to recognize and operate only under their rightful owner, products will be much more difficult for thieves to steal. For instance, a car stereo will operate only within the car in which it was installed originally.

Not all sensors will be the result of nanotechnology. In fact, today's MEMS-based sensors are already gaining widespread use in a variety of applications—including in automobiles, where they are being used in everything from air bags to tires—and are already taking us down the path of miniaturization. As the sensors become smaller, cheaper, more powerful, and capable of interacting with a variety of other products and systems, daily life will substantially change as the things around us behave with intelligence. (The difference from the applications discussed in the previous chapter will not so much be in how these sensors are being used, but rather in the scale of their use. By 2009, the price will be so low that they will be ubiquitous.)

Businesses that rely heavily on inventory control will be among the early beneficiaries because these nanosensors will not only be able to track a product from the moment it is created to the time it leaves the warehouse but, ultimately, to when it is discarded. Inventory control will slowly become a fading issue for manufacturers as just-in-time manufacturing becomes the norm. These nanosensors will even be able to communicate important information back to both the manufacturers and the users. For example, a carton of milk will be able to "sense" if it has been exposed to warm temperatures for too long and will alert the consumer that the milk is no longer good. A stereo set will be able to "sense" if it was damaged in the delivery process. Tiny sensors in your socks may even tell the washing machine how hot or cold to make the water.

Integrated nanosensor systems capable of collecting, processing, and communicating massive amounts of data with minimal size, weight, and power consumption will allow for real-time pricing information. For example, a "smart" refrigerator, discussed in chapter six, will not only know to run its compressor during nonpeak energy hours, it will also be able to "talk" with the milk carton to find out if is getting low and, if so, it can relay that information to your PDA, which will remind you to pick up a carton of milk next time you swing by the store. A sophisticated system will even be able to relay that information to the store, which in turn can pass on the information to the milk distributor, who will ensure that the product is available when you need it—and the store will have every item on your grocery list waiting for you to pick up.

Still other nanosensors will detect for food-borne pathogens. The strategic deployment of nanosensors in the more than six thousand meatpacking plants scattered around the United States or at the ports and border crossings through which foreign fruits and vegetables enter the country can potentially eradicate a sizeable percentage of the millions of food-borne illnesses that afflict people every year. These nanosensors can even alleviate the workload of (and need for) a number of the state, local, and federal government food inspectors while improving the public's confidence in the safety of their food.

A related application will be to use such devices for sensing when crops are at the optimal ripeness for picking. For example, a tomato farmer will no longer have to rely on instinct to know when to harvest his crop. Instead, using a hand-held device, he could prick a tomato and determine whether it was the optimal time for picking. Such devices could also eliminate some of the guesswork of trying to pick a "good" cantaloupe at the grocery store.

New cars will contain chips with nanosensors that can track pollution with pinpoint accuracy and report that information to a local control agency. (The public's concern about the misuse or abuse of nanosensors is a real issue and should not be discounted. Just because the application is possible does not mean that it will gain acceptance in the marketplace.) Businesses that emit pollution will be similarly tracked. The implications for public policymakers are vast. Instead of relying on command-and-control systems to regulate pollution, government administrators will be able to forego the burdensome, inefficient approaches of the past and instead rely on precise, real-time information to assess costs. Those businesses and vehicles that pollute excessively will be charged accordingly.

Economists have consistently demonstrated that market-based pricing mechanisms—pricing systems that reflect the true cost of a product—are superior tools for reducing pollution. For example, this is why some states choose to impose a nickel or dime incentive for recycling soda and beers containers . . . because some people will change their behavior. Such pricing mechanisms also have the added benefit of applying a profit motive to companies to find innovative solutions to reduce pollution and thus save money. (Just imagine if the owner of a large diesel truck is charged for the exact amount of black soot the vehicle spews out. If the price is set high enough, the owner will find a way to reduce the pollution.)

As cheap sensors become ubiquitous, a variety of new applications will emerge. If car usage can be tracked by the mile, insurance companies need not base your insurance rate on static information like the price of your car or the zip code of the town you live in. Instead, your rate could be determined by the precise number of miles you drive as well as when and where you drive. If you avoid driving during rush hour, for example, when accidents are more likely, your rates would reflect this fact. The implications are wider still, because if government chooses to employ such sensors to tax road usage or pollution, companies will modify their behavior to maximize profits.

AGRICULTURE

Nanosensors for DNA testing will not only impact human disease diagnosis, they will also allow agricultural specialists to understand plant genetics better. For example, if specific genes are expressed when a plant is exposed to any number of things—such as salt or drought—and scientists and researchers can understand the process, they can develop plants that require less water, can grow in harsh conditions, or even use salt water instead of freshwater.

The implications of any of these developments will be significant. China, India, Pakistan, and a large portion of the western United States—all large agricultural producers—suffer from a shortage of freshwater. If crops can be produced that minimize the amount of freshwater required, farmers and agribusiness can remain profitable in those areas.

If new crops can be grown in different climates, the global balance of trade might change significantly. For example, if the finest wines of France, Chile, and Australia can be replicated with grapes grown in Africa or Russia, what are the implications for winemakers around the world? What happens to the wine-importing business?

In addition to the wider benefit of a greater food supply, world prices may be reduced and transportation costs minimized as more crops are grown closer to market. Nanosensors will help this development take hold by allowing fertilizer and insecticides to be applied only to those areas where they are absolutely needed.

Another huge area where nanotechnology will manifest itself is that of tailored agriculture production. Currently $80 billion worth of plant oil is used every year in the production of plastics, paints, and other products. The problem, from the perspective of the users of these products, is that the oils must first be modified using expensive chemical-processing plants. Agricultural researchers are now, however, working to change plant enzymes so that the plants make the exact type of oil needed in the first place. Instead of using expensive, environmentally unfriendly processes that rely on chemicals and high temperatures and high pressures to refine plant oils, the plants can instead be manipulated to use their own natural molecular processes to create refined oil. Why pay for chemicals and additives when something can be done for free?

Still another significant growth area will be in the enhancement of products to improve nutrition and health— to the point of producing edible vaccines. Currently in the United States, children must endure a number of painful vaccination shots. Compliance is less than perfect because many people don't like shots. Others don't get the necessary shots because the equipment is expensive and access limited. There are other associated problems with vaccines, including the risk that the syringes will spread disease and the vaccines may spoil due to lack of refrigeration, although the latter problems are more likely to occur in third-world countries. Nanotechnology-enabled advances will alleviate many of the problems by incorporating the vaccine right into an edible product. For example, corn could be modified to contain the vaccine for hepatitis B. If successful, as many as one million people who die annually of hepatitis B around the world due to a lack of vaccine could be saved.

ENERGY

Every day more than enough sunlight strikes the planet to meet the energy needs of the entire world. Harvesting this energy has been possible for decades. The challenge, however, has been in converting the sun's energy efficiently into electricity.

Nanotechnology will address this issue by advancing solar-cell technology. As we better understand how electrical charges move at the nanoscale, new nanomaterials and nanodevices (in the form of nanolayers or nanorods) will be developed that channel and amplify this action, resulting in better conversion from solar energy (light) to electrical energy. To understand the ramifications, consider that today's best solar cells convert approximately 35 percent of sunlight into energy. When this percentage is increased to 50 percent or greater, solar energy suddenly becomes a viable energy alternative even in cloud-covered northern cities. This will be especially true because nanotechnology advances in the area of new materials will help replace expensive silicon (which is used to build today's best solar cells) with low-cost nanomaterials.

Advances in fuel cells, described in chapter five, will also continue to improve during this time frame. With one-third of the world still having no access to centrally generated electricity, the large-scale commercialization of small, portable fuel cells has the potential to fundamentally alter the energy paradigm: People will no longer need to be tied to large, centrally located energy grids. Furthermore, fuel cells, by virtue of their ability to both produce and store energy, will allow homes and businesses (even cars, potentially) to become net energy producers. Imagine the consequences if you not only don't have to buy any energy from your local power supplier, but you can resell some of your excess back to the company or your neighbor.

Thermoelectric energy, electricity generated by heat, has been a dream for efficient energy generation for many years, and nanotech may make it a reality. Recently scientists at multiple labs have fabricated unique semiconducting nanomaterials to create proto-type thermoelectric materials. One of the first applications will be to use the heat from an engine's exhaust to generate electricity. This electricity can be used to operate the car more efficiently (hybrid engines) or perhaps cook a meal on a camping trip.

Within the decade, Mike Roco, senior advisor for nanotechnology at the NSF, projects that nanotechnology-based lighting advances have the potential to reduce worldwide consumption of energy by 10 percent. This will represent a savings of more than $100 billion and will reduce by 200 million tons the amount of carbon dioxide pumped into the air.

This is possible because many companies and researchers are exploiting nanotechnology's potential. Home-lighting systems employing nanosensors will be able to track occupants and supply light only when and where needed, saving big money by reducing energy usage worldwide. Other researchers are using molecular organic films to create flexible layers of light-emitting diodes. When an electric field is applied to these films, a soft glow results. Suddenly you have light fixtures that are more like paint or wallpaper. Developed in 2002 by GE, the technology will have advanced sufficiently and be cheap enough to find its way to the marketplace by the end of the decade.

NANOPOINTS

* Will your business be impacted if significant advances are made in the treatment of AIDS, diabetes, or obesity or in drug, tobacco, or alcohol treatment?
* What aspect(s) of your business can benefit from cheap sensors? Are there environmental conditions (e.g., temperature, humidity, pollution) or health conditions (e.g., smoke, gas, bacteria, pollen, mold, etc.) that you or your customers would benefit from knowing about?
* How will your business be affected by changes in how and where agricultural products are grown?
* If nanotechnology-enabled advances bring low-cost, accessible electricity to even a small portion of the 1.8 billion people around the world without reliable energy, do new markets open up for you and your business?
* Have fuel cells reached a point where they are an economically viable alternative to your present energy needs?
* Have solar cells become efficient enough to be installed on your home or building?

CHAPTER EIGHT

2013 & Beyond: The World Becomes Smaller and Smarter

"ANY SUFFICIENTLY ADVANCED TECHNOLOGY IS INDISTINGUISHABLE FROM MAGIC."

—ARTHUR C. CLARKE, AUTHOR OF *2001: A SPACE ODYSSEY*

In 1913, Lee De Forest was prosecuted for mail fraud for claiming to potential investors that RCA would be able to transmit the human voice across the Atlantic in a few years. The "father of the radio" and the inventor of the audion tube, a device that improved radio-signal amplification, De Forest had run up against a wall of disbelief in technology. The prosecuting attorney in the case stated that "based on these absurd and misleading statements, the misguided public has been persuaded to purchase stock in his company." De Forest was acquitted and the case was thrown out, but not before the judge admonished him to not make any more outlandish claims.

It is possible that by 2013 people and businesses will make similar claims against self-repairing materials, solar cells painted on buildings, cars that drive themselves, a human heart that grows itself, unlimited clean water, and even a process that reverses aging. Yet all of these claims, like De Forest's claim about transmitting the human voice across the Atlantic, are based on sound science and are likely to come to fruition.

SPACE

"Space: The final frontier." Most of us are familiar with the popular *Star Trek* phrase and intuitively believe it because the great unknown is a powerful motivator. The need to see, feel, and understand unexplored areas has charted the history of mankind. It is what drives many of the men and women at NASA today—and their work has led to the development of Teflon, stronger and lighter materials and glues, water-purification systems, remote temperature sensing, advanced computer modeling for thermal and vibration assessments, the laptop computer, and self-repairing windshields.

To explore space, NASA has always needed several things: (1) stronger and lighter materials that can perform multiple functions, (2) self-repairing systems or materials, (3) equipment with low power requirements and efficient means of generating power, (4) miniaturized parts and equipment, (5) powerful computers, and (6) good health care.

All of these requirements will continue to boost the understanding and development of technology—especially nanotechnology—here on earth. And as nanotechnology is developed and then applied to the harsh environment of space, commercial applications on earth will abound.

Nanotechnology is already leading to a revolution in material science, but NASA's needs are likely to push the envelope of material development even further. Materials with the toughness and durability of diamonds but lighter than aluminum are a real possibility. As NASA continues to champion the development and production of these materials, the price will likely continue to drop, and the analogy in chapter four of materials moving from space applications to very high-end niches (e.g. NASCAR and America's Cup yacht racing) to high-end markets (Lexus, Jaguar, etc.) to everyday products (e.g. kitchen appliances, bikes, and toys) will be very real.

In addition to requiring new materials that simply minimize weight or increase strength, NASA will need materials to perform several functions simultaneously. Currently aluminum is widely used for multiple purposes. It serves as the structure and provides mechanical stability, it acts as a heat conductor to keep the spacecraft in thermal equilibrium, and it shields equipment and occupants against the radiation of space. By 2013, nanotechnology-generated composite materials will be able not only to perform these functions at a fraction of aluminum's weight, but also to provide additional capabilities like wireless communication and the conversion of heat into electricity.

Many of the trips NASA is planning will last years, decades, or even longer. Mishaps and accidents will inevitably occur, and the normal presence of space particles (like micrometeorites) that constantly bombard space vehicles will wear on the spacecraft. If the spacecraft are to survive and function on these longer missions, they will need to repair themselves. By embedding nanosensors and energy sources directly into new nanomaterials, these

materials can become self-repairing. Through the application of an external force such as heat, a material's molecular composition can configure itself into its original
shape without the loss of physical integrity. For any business that deals with the materials (whether it be steel,
plastic, aluminum, ceramics, textiles, or composites), the
implications are astounding. If cars, bridges, buildings,
windows, and clothes can suddenly be made to self-repair,
what happens to the classic business model? How will
businesses generate new sales if their products are lasting
longer? What happens to the service contracts and repair
revenue that are currently associated with those items?
The flip side is that entirely new products will be possible, and new applications for existing products will
emerge since the products can serve a wider variety of
uses and withstand far more stressing environments.

The long trips NASA is planning will also require substantially more energy, and it will become necessary to harvest some of that energy from space. By creating devices
and materials that allow energy to be collected, stored, and
applied more efficiently, nanotechnology can address this
important need. Nanotechnology-enabled solar cells based
on nanorods embedded in plastic, such as those under
development at the University of California at Berkeley
today, will be much more efficient by 2013. As NASA and
others develop this solar-cell technology, solar cells here on
earth will also benefit.

If the efficiency of the plastic solar cells increases
enough, and if the price drops enough, it is entirely possible that solar cells can be brushed in layers onto almost
any product that requires power. This means that a phone
or even a building will not need a battery, a fuel cell, or
any external energy source because it will be able to

power itself from the energy it collects from the sun. In fact, it is believed that due to nanotechnology, solar cells will become so effective that they will be able to operate off the light in a room. Another application might be solar-powered clothing. If nanorods can be embedded in plastics, they most likely can be embedded in clothing. And if super chips can also be embedded in the clothing, then the idea of "wearing" a computer is no longer so strange.

NASA's requirement for smaller spacecraft, a need driven by its desire to lower the cost of launching satellites, will support the above-mentioned developments of lighter composite materials and better power sources. It will also lead to the making of gears and parts at the molecular level. For example, if microsatellites need a motor to move antennas, deploy probes, or adjust solar panels in the deep cold of outer space, nanoscale gears, which require no lubrication, may be a necessary enabling technology. The continued miniaturization of parts and gears will have a host of applications for businesses. For instance, if nanoscale gears can enable nanoscale motors, a number of products can be made smaller, and because no lubrication is required, these parts will likely last longer and perform more efficiently.

NASA's need for miniaturization will also drive the development of nanoelectronics. Smaller, more powerful, and more fault-tolerant computers are needed for long and complex space missions. And if the computers can become small enough and smart enough, they can eliminate the need for the astronaut. Longer, riskier, and more fruitful trips (in terms of data-collection) are thus possible. The NASA Mars program intends to use unmanned systems (many using extensive nanotechnology approaches) to first assess and study Mars, then potentially send small factories to produce oxygen and water on the red planet in anticipation of the first human setting foot there.

The military has long been working on unmanned jet fighters and bombers. More powerful, smaller computers, enabled by nanoelectronics, will not only avoid putting humans at risk, but as the computers get smarter and more sophisticated they may outperform humans and become more effective weapons or surveillance vehicles.

Airlines have known for some time that computers can safely fly and even land planes. In many circumstances, they can actually perform better, although pilots and customers alike are uncomfortable giving control over to a computer. If, however, the public sees computer-operated jet fighters perform successfully in war, it might become more comfortable with the idea of a plane having only one pilot instead of two or three. After all, if an industry such as shipping, which is largely out of the public's sight, can employ computers, sensors, and other equipment to load cargo and navigate a ship automatically (as it is already doing), why not the airplane and, ultimately, the automobile industry?

Although the idea of turning your car over to a computer may sound like science fiction, for future generations (especially those that will have grown up with smart toys and interactive computer games) it may seem like common sense. Many of us know people who still use typewriters. They do so not because they dispute the superiority of the word processor, but rather because they are set in their ways and comfortable with typing on mechanical keys. People who manually drive their car might be viewed in the same light in the future.

Space will not, however, only be the domain of small

unpiloted spacecraft built out of super materials and run by supercomputers. Man is curious by nature, and humans will want to explore space further themselves. To do so, significant health-care issues will need to be addressed.

One of the most serious issues confronting NASA and any astronaut who travels into space—especially for long periods—is radiation. Currently, if an astronaut is exposed for too long to the radiation of space, radiation sickness and cell damage (from cosmic rays) can occur. These radiation interactions can change the way cells operate, damage the DNA of a cell, and potentially cause it to become cancerous or nonfunctioning. To address this issue, researchers at NASA are looking to nanotechnology as the way to enter damaged cells and either repair or kill them. NASA is highly motivated to develop such a solution. This is true not just for radiation damage but for any number of health-care issues. If a human gets sick in space, returning to earth for treatment will often not be a viable option.

THE HUMAN BODY SHOP

Nanotechnology, as discussed in the previous chapters, is already making great advances in health care. By the middle of the next decade, medicine will be on the verge of seismic change.

Many of us will ultimately die from some type of organ failure. This fact and the fact that seventy-six million baby-boomers are quickly approaching the age when such failures begin to occur will drive the medical market to continue a search for a solution to this problem. And the boomers' financial wherewithal to pay for any new technology that aids in the development of a solution could push nanotechnology to the market faster than expected.

The body's largest organ is the skin. Medical researchers have already made great progress in growing new skin, and in 2002 the FDA approved one such process. Other researchers are now working on growing a bladder. In the not-too-distant future, the kidney and the liver will become candidates for regrowth. Eventually it might even be possible to grow a heart. In fact, NASA is working on growing tiny patches of heart tissue. Using tiny scaffolds, the researchers are able to collect heart cells and get them to connect with one another, and the cells have even begun to beat like a full-grown heart when placed in a bioreactor, a device that mimics the condition of the human body and allows cells to grow (or "self-associate") in three-dimensional patterns.

The immediate application of these technologies will be to address the severe shortage of organs that confronts the medical community today. The waiting list for people desiring an organ is 80,000, and more than 6,000 people die every year in the U.S. from failure to obtain an organ. Combine these numbers with the fact that current organ transplants are expensive, invasive, and often relegate the person receiving the transplant to a strict regimen of drugs, and the incentive to address the issue is clear. As doctors begin to understand how to manipulate the right cells into the right places, they will be able to repair the damaged organs and, ultimately, grow new ones.

This development will be profound. If heart disease, the leading cause of death in the United States, can be prevented, what will be the impact on life expectancy? And if organ regrowth becomes possible, one of the most likely scenarios is that the life span will increase. Modern medicine has done a wonderful job of increasing the life expectancy of people. To date, however, no progress has been made in expanding the ultimate length of life. The world's oldest people tend to be around 100 to 115 years old. Nanotechnology and other medical advances will thus likely not only increase the number of people living above 100 but push the upper limit to 120 years and beyond.

Our ability to regrow cells is perhaps the ultimate in nanomedicine because of its implications for growing old. Aging occurs when cells can no longer divide, and this occurs when the telomeres, the physical ends of chromosomes that serve important protection and replication functions, shrink. (Think of telomeres as imposing a finite life on cells.) If telomerase, an enzyme that rebuilds telomeres, can be reproduced and introduced into the body to repair cells, then the clock on the life of cells and organs can not only be slowed, it can be *reset.* Instead of viewing aging as an inevitable development—something to be endured—aging would be viewed as a disease and thus something to be treated. (The moral, ethical, cultural, and societal issues that these changes will evoke are significant. How society will react to these changes is discussed further in chapter nine.) The implications of such a paradigm shift are huge.

Other medical advances likely to show great promise beyond 2013 include the following:

- **Chromosome-replacement therapy.** Extracting existing chromosomes from diseased cells and replacing them with new, healthy, manufactured chromosomes will create healthy cells and could provide a permanent cure to any number of genetic diseases, including cystic fibrosis, hemophilia, sickle cell anemia, and Huntington's.

- **Neuron encapsulation.** Neurons could be encapsulated and planted in the brain and electrically stimulated to release neurotransmitters to treat Alzheimer's patients or spinal cord injuries.

- **Artificial red blood cells.** Poor blood flow and inadequate oxygen supply are major causes of tissue damage. Heart attack and stroke victims often suffer far greater damage due to a lack of oxygen than from any problem caused by the initial attack. Artificial red blood cells, which would be injected into the body, hold great promise in addressing this problem. They would work like this: Imagine a tiny sphere (approximately one hundred nanometers) filled with high-pressure oxygen. The sphere, likely a tailor-made nanomaterial with specific-sized pores, would release oxygen molecules at a constant rate to provide the body with enough oxygen until the body can begin producing oxygen itself. These artificial red blood cells, referred to as respirocytes, could also enhance human performance. Imagine runners or soldiers who could sprint for minutes at a time or lifeguards who could search underwater for an extended period without scuba gear. (It is not difficult to imagine a variety of new ethical issues revolving around the use of these devices in sports in the same way steroids and other performance-enhancing drugs are already widely debated.)

The bottom line is that the entire health-care industry is in for an era of unprecedented change. The mapping of the human genome, a better understanding of protein folding, and vastly more sophisticated equipment will allow the medical professionals of tomorrow to treat disease at the molecular level—the level where life and death actually occur. The profession will change from one of medical science to one of medical engineering—to repairing, restoring, and rebuilding the body at the molecular level. Diseases and illnesses that once seemed commonplace and natural will be eradicated and will appear as foreign to future generations as polio and syphilis seem to today's baby-boomers.

CREATIVE COMPUTERS

Between 2015 and 2020, the power of the new nanoelectronics-based computers will approach the capability of the human brain. Whether they are made from nanomaterials or are truly molecular-based nanoelectronic machines, these computers will offer significant improvement for high-performance speed, power, and memory density while reducing power usage by a factor of up to fifty. The merger of nanosensors, nanoelectronics, and nanomaterials will continue the creation of better and more sophisticated virtual-reality (or augmented-reality) stations. Applications may include everything from individualized learning stations tailored to each student's needs to business-related applications that allow customers to try out and modify products from the comfort of their homes. For example, instead of simply reading text, students learning about chemistry will be able to augment their lesson by not only watching a video of a chemical reaction but by experiencing how the molecules move, change, and adhere to one another in 3-D. Customers who are virtually touring a home—something that can be done today on the two-dimensional domain of the Internet—will not only be able to do it in 3-D, they might even be able to "touch" and "smell" products. (The ability to "touch" something might be done by simulating neurons in the brain, while "smelling" something might be replicated by releasing molecules that mirror the smell of the original product.) Any business that sells its products through the traditional brick-and-mortar setting may be impacted. Virtual or augmented reality, unlike the Internet, may permit customers to "kick the tires." It is possible that people will still prefer to shop at brick-and-mortar shops for a variety of reasons, but businesses should be aware of potential threats.

The raw ability of these machines to process, analyze, and make decisions based on the information provided will mean that machines are likely to do as well as if not better than their human counterparts in analyzing and selecting stocks. If so, stockbrokers and mutual-fund managers, who are already feeling the pressure of powerful computers and sophisticated analytical software, will need to continue to rethink how they can add value to their customers. In the future, it is also likely that computers will become creative in the sense that they will be able to analyze problems and come up with unique solutions because they can efficiently access an untold number of databases.

Think of it this way. It presently takes an average of thirteen years to educate someone to receive a high-school diploma, an additional four years to get a bachelor's degree, and another two to three years for a master's degree. A computer will be able to download an equivalent amount of information almost instantly. How all of this information will be applied is difficult to fathom, but the reality is that machine intelligence is growing exponentially, and many jobs and industries will be affected.

Professionals, especially those employed as part of the "knowledge economy"—people who process and synthesize large amounts of information—will need to rethink how they can add value to the customer. For example, if computers can provide everything from legal, medical, and educational information, lawyers, doctors, and teachers need to reconsider how they approach their work. While it is possible that these machines may replace some workers, it may also be the case that the devices encourage more people to go into "human" professions like teaching and nursing because the computers will free them to concentrate on the truly "human" aspects of those jobs.

"GLOBAL SALVATION"?

The United Nations estimates that there are thirty-eight global trouble spots where fighting might break out due to water shortage. If nanofiltration systems can desalinize water, or if nanotechnology-enabled advances can reduce water usage, or if nanobiotechnology can help grow crops in either drought conditions or with salt water, competing populations would no longer have to fight for control over scarce resources. A significant number of global conflicts might be avoided. Couple these developments with nanotechnology-enabled advances in energy production (fuel cells and solar cells), computer power, and health-care advances (e.g., edible vaccines, disease prevention, etc.) and it is within the realm of possibility that vast portions of the world's population will have adequate access to energy, education, and health care within the next twenty years.

Famine, disease, war, and illiteracy have plagued the developing world for centuries, and they might continue to do so for some time. But by making so many things faster, better, stronger, and cheaper, nanotechnology has the real potential to address these serious global issues.

If such predictions seem to stretch credibility, consider that most experts are predicting nanotechnology to usher in more change in the next twenty years than we have seen in the last one hundred years. And then consider that one hundred years ago in the United States, life expectancy was forty-seven years, there were only 8,000 cars and 144 miles of paved road, 95 percent of births occurred at home, pneumonia and influenza were the leading causes of death, and only 6 percent of Americans graduated from high school. In this light, nanotechnology's ability to transform a world seems not only plausible but downright likely.

SELF-ASSEMBLERS

The one nanotechnology development that you will likely read and hear a good deal about but that is not likely anytime soon (within twenty years) is something called the self-assembler. Nanotechnology visionaries see a day when a machine can take the raw feedstock of nature—atoms—and build virtually anything. For example, rather than having a cow eat grass and drink water and process the atoms into a filet mignon, a machine would simply mix an exact ratio of the same atoms found in grass and water and construct the steak for you.

The vision is this: Build a device, sometimes referred to as a nanobot, that can pick up, move, and place atoms into a precise location. Then instruct this nanobot to build an exact replica of itself. Repeat this process a number of times—two, four, eight, sixteen—and eventually you can create a huge number of these devices. They, in turn, can begin building almost anything known to man today (e.g., phones, computers, cars, etc.), most of which consist of trillions or quadrillions of atoms. Proponents envision a world free from material want because anyone will be able to build anything. Opponents, on the other hand, fear these devices will get out of hand and disassemble anything in their path. This scenario is often referred to as the "gray goo" problem. (The term is meant to reflect the fact that these nanobots could theoretically turn all matter into an amorphous glob of disassembled atoms.)

While there is serious science behind the vision (visit www.foresight.org for more information), the reality is much more complicated and makes the possibility of such devices fairly remote. First, at the atomic level it will require a great deal of energy to put together or pull apart atoms. Thus, the question of a power source must be adequately addressed. (If adequately addressed, the question of a power source might also ease concerns of the gray goo scenario because, in theory, the power source could be kept independent of the nanobot and be controlled only by humans.)

The second and more fundamental problem is that which has been dubbed the "fat fingers" problem. In short, any device that pinches or holds atoms will have to be made out of atoms itself. And because every atom reacts to and is dependent on the other atoms around it, it is not enough to simply place an atom exactly where you want it. You must hold all the other atoms around it in place. The problem is obvious: If you have to hold multiple atoms together simultaneously but the devices that you must use are larger than the components you are holding, it becomes impossible. (Picture trying to build a

Swiss watch, with its tiny mechanical parts, using only your fingers.)

The third and final problem, which is referred to as the "sticky fingers" problem, relates to something called "striction," a combination of friction and stickiness. Because of their large surface area, the atoms being moved will likely stick to the "assembler" hand, making it extremely difficult to place the atoms precisely where they need to go. (The problem is comparable to trying to build the same Swiss watch, only now your hands are covered with glue.)

Do all of these problems mean the self-assembler is impossible? No. Difficult? Probably. But don't dismiss it out of hand. After all, Mother Nature has overcome the fat finger and the sticky finger problems to create the ultimate in self-assembly: human life. Furthermore, Zyvex Corporation has pulled together a world-class team of researchers and is working on a self-assembler. The work is apparently so promising that the U.S. government, rather than claiming it to be fraudulent, has provided the company a $25 million grant . . . a step that would likely make Lee De Forest proud.

NANOPOINTS

* Do you keep an open mind when you hear about futuristic developments, or do you laugh off such ideas as fraudulent, outlandish, or impossible?
* Is anyone in your organization responsible for tracking developments coming out of NASA?
* What are the implications for your product or your business if materials can be embedded with their own power source?

* If computers and sensors become so sophisticated that people's comfort level reaches a point where they begin to turn over to computers functions such as driving cars and flying planes, how will your business be impacted?

* If quality life expectancy drastically increases, for example from eighty years to ninety-five years, what would be the impact on your business? How will the sales of your products be affected if more people are living longer and more productive lives?

* If you are in the health-care industry, how do you construct a long-term, sustainable business model that is based on prevention as opposed to the treatment of disease?

* What would it mean for your business if two billion people in the developing world had access to adequate supplies of food, energy, and education?

* If 800,000 nanotechnology workers will be needed within the decade, are there steps your business should be taking today to prepare for this reality? Do any of the universities or colleges in your area offer courses in nanotechnology? Are your local grade schools and high schools providing their students (your workers of tomorrow) the requisite background in physics, chemistry, biology, and computational sciences to compete for the high-paying jobs of tomorrow?

CHAPTER NINE

And in Conclusion . . . This Is Just the Beginning

"PEOPLE MUST START THINKING IN UNCONVENTIONAL
WAYS IF WE ARE TO TAKE FULL ADVANTAGE OF THE
OPPORTUNITIES IN THIS NEW AND REVOLUTIONARY
FIELD."

—THE INTERAGENCY WORKING GROUP ON
NANOSCIENCE, ENGINEERING AND TECHNOLOGY

The dynamic and unexpected interactions between nanotechnology-enabled advances in computers, materials, sensors, energy, communication, and medicine will lead to hundreds of new products and marketplace applications—many of which are beyond the ability of anyone to predict realistically today. The task of trying to predict precisely how nanotechnology will impact business is further complicated because every new technology also interacts (and sometimes collides) with powerful social customs, government regulations, and people's comfort level with technology. For example, just because the inventors and manufacturers of a wearable device that can simultaneously act as a computer, a communication device, and a personal health monitor think it is the greatest thing since sliced bread, if it makes the user look like a cyborg, the product might fail in the marketplace because it is viewed as "socially unacceptable." (Although what is socially unacceptable in one place at one time could quickly become the norm. Just try to remember your reaction the first time you saw someone speaking on a cell phone in a public place in the early 1990s.)

THE POWER OF THE STATUS QUO

Contrary to the famous old saying, the world does not always beat a path to the door of those who build a better mousetrap. In fact, the world is littered with seemingly superior technologies, from keyboards that allow people to type faster, to Beta's alleged superiority over VHS, to Drucker's automobiles of the 1950s, to many of today's software programs that must compete against Microsoft's marketplace dominance. Nanotechnologies of all types will face similar battles.

Many nanotechnologies, for example, will not take off for the simple reason that they do not provide consumers *enough* of a reason to change their behavior. This is especially true in the nanomaterial market. Superior performance in terms of a lighter, stronger, or more recyclable material might be beneficial to the end user, but if it costs more, calls for the customer to change behavior, or requires the manufacturer to modify his manufacturing process significantly, it might not find a home in the marketplace.

For example, NEC (Nippon Electronics Corporation) has used carbon nanotubes to build a fuel cell with ten times the energy density of today's most advanced batteries. The fuel cell holds the potential to replace the batteries in cell phones and laptops. The problem is that this will require a shift on the part of the consumer, who would have to change from recharging his phone (something he is used to) to the concept of refilling his phone with hydrogen.

This is the one of the hurdles of nanotechnology. While the technology might lead to a better product, if the consumer is unwilling to change, it might be relegated to the ash heap of a thousand other better mousetraps. For example, fuel-cell phones might be a superior product, but if nanotechnology advances can also improve batteries to a level that is even close to the performance level of fuel cells, the consumer may not want to be bothered with changing his behavior.

Government will be a second force to be reckoned with. If government regulators cannot determine, to some level of certainty, what long-term impacts different nano-medical applications have on human health or what effect certain nanoparticles have on the environment, the regulators could prohibit their use until more definitive information is forthcoming. These regulators could easily be joined by other powerful political constituencies who have a vested financial interest in ensuring that new nanotechnologies do not disrupt their current business. Working separately or together, these forces could delay or kill a number of promising nanotechnology applications. For example, it is not difficult to imagine the pharmaceutical industry spending big money to discredit a new nanotechnology that threatens its business or the oil and gas industry lobbying against new energy technologies.

CHANGE IS NEVER EASY

The most difficult variable in trying to determine the path of any new technology is how people will react to it. From the weavers who were replaced by the looming mills to the carriage makers who were replaced by the automobile, history is filled with examples of people first fearing—and even attacking—new technologies that threatened their livelihood and way of life.

Nanotechnology will be no different. Change is coming for a lot of people and industries. The difference with nanotechnology is that the scope of what it will make possible and the speed with which it will change things far exceed all the technologies that have preceded it. The new materials of tomorrow will not just be improvements on the materials that man has extracted from the earth. They will be entirely new materials that even Mother Nature herself could not invent.

For the sizeable portion of the population that believes Mother Nature knows best (and thus should not be messed with), man's rapid journey into this arena is fraught with danger and should be avoided at all costs. Some religions already oppose technology on philosophical grounds, and other religions are struggling with some of the moral and ethical issues technology is already imposing. These people's worldview will inevitably clash with those who have a more "technology-friendly" perspective—people who believe that if man can do it, he should do it. The debates swirling around stem cells and human cloning are just two current examples. Nanotechnology is only going to add further fuel to the flame.

The battle between these diametrically opposed perspectives will likely be fought in the public-policy arena. Who will win is impossible to determine. And even if those who oppose new nanotechnologies are successful in the public arena, it is no guarantee that individuals, corporations, or other countries won't press ahead with developments anyway. (Which is precisely what is happening in the field of stem-cell research today.) The ethical considerations alone are staggering. Advances in nanomedicine have the potential to alter how we view ourselves and our lives in ways that are difficult to fathom. As discussed in the previous chapter, nanotechnology may not just slow the aging process, it might *reverse* it. How people will react to such seismic change cannot be anticipated. Nowhere will these clashes between two groups be more evident than in the area of health care.

WHICH PATH TO TAKE (OR FOLLOW)?

In addition to the confusing tangle of large-scale political implications of nanotechnology, which will be played out at a level beyond where most businesses can make an impact, nanotechnology will also be difficult to factor into your long-term planning scenarios at a more immediate level. The reason is that more than one nanotechnology-enabled solution will exist to most problems.

The issue will be further complicated because the best technology might not necessarily win. For example, multiple nanotechnology-enabled solutions will exist to treat diabetes. One solution may be for diabetics to wear small patches laced with nanoprobes that can painlessly prick the skin, sample blood, and administer insulin as necessary. Another viable solution might be to use nano-sensors embedded in the body and then administer insulin, in the form of nanoparticles in nanocapsules, on an as-needed basis. A third option might be simply to grow a new pancreas.

Which one will win will not be determined by cost and convenience alone. Government regulation, insurance policies, people's reluctance to change, and even individuals' comfort level with technology must all be considered. It is entirely possible that all three solutions (as well as others) will peacefully coexist in a fragmented market.

Such is the case with energy. Longer-lasting and more powerful batteries enabled by advances in nanotechnology will battle with fuel cells, which will battle with solar cells, which will fight with nuclear power for a share of the energy market. All will be improved by nanotechnology, and all are likely to continue to find large and small marketplace applications. Safety, government policies, local preferences, and local conditions will all factor in determining which technology wins.

NEW PARADIGMS

As difficult as all of these challenges are, they pale in comparison with how people and businesses will need to think differently. The rules of the game are about to change. Paradigms are shifting and competitors are springing from new quarters.

Nanomedical applications will force the health-care and pharmaceutical industries to change from a paradigm of viewing disease as something to be *treated* to something that must be *prevented.*

Energy suppliers will be forced by nanotechnology-enabled advances in fuel cells and solar cells to view homeowners not just as customers but as potential competitors (because they will be able to produce their own power independently).

Manufacturers, in the new era of nanomaterials, will have to shift from providing their customers a "catalogue of products" to first asking them what their *precise* needs are. They will then need to build products to those specifications.

Nanoelectronics will force the electronics industry to shift away from using multibillion-dollar chip-fabrication plants to build ever-finer circuits and find new ways to build the computers of tomorrow. They may even have to "grow" circuits for the new computers.

Academic disciplines will blur and spawn into new areas of study as advances in biology, physics, chemistry, and computational science feed into each other in unexpected ways. Education will become constant, and the rapid advancement of knowledge will require the $680 billion education industry to adapt or become irrelevant.

And almost every industry will have to come to terms with the confluence of powerful computers; cheap, ubiquitous sensors; and the ability to communicate and transfer rapidly vast amounts of data that nanotechnology will enable.

FINAL NANOTHOUGHTS

A survey of nanotechnology experts at a workshop sponsored by the National Science Foundation suggests that the probability of the type of commercial applications covered in this book actually occurring within the next fifteen to twenty years is quite high, with the majority of applications falling within the 90 to 100 percent category.

This means the question is not *if* nanotechnology is going to happen but *when*. Nanotechnology is fueling advances all across the modern industrial spectrum, and things are happening today. And advances that might be thought of as being ten years away today could, as a result of new developments, be only five years away tomorrow.

It is therefore not too soon to begin thinking about how you and your business will be required to change in the years ahead. Because in many ways nanotechnology is not just going to be the next big thing . . . it is going to be *everything*.

NOTES

Unless noted otherwise, industry statistics were obtained from 2001 and 2002 issues of *Value Line Investment Survey,* published monthly by Value Line Publishers, Inc., New York, NY. The amounts stated are the estimated 2002 revenue values.

Introduction

page 11: These are not the predictions: M. C. Roco, R. S. Williams, and P. Alivisatos, *Nanotechnology Research Directions: IWGN Workshop Report,* Kluwer Academic Publishers, 2000.

page 11: Less than a decade: Christopher Cerf and Victor Navasky, *The Experts Speak:* Villard, 1998.

page 13: within the decade: "Nanotech initiative will focus next year on developing instruments, advisor says," United Press International, February 11, 2002.

page 13: Before 2010: Otis Port and Roger O. Crockett, "Nano Technology," *BusinessWeek,* April 1, 2002, p. 181.

page 14: This is up from 45: Amanda Gome, "The Atomic Revolution," *Business Weekly Review,* p. 68.

page 14: "The impact of nanotechnology . . .": Richard Smalley, "National Nanotechnology Initiative: Leading to the Next Industrial Revolution," National Science and Technology Council, Committee on Technology. Supplement to the president's FY2001 budget, February 2000.

page 14: "Because of nanotechnology . . .": Mike Roco quoted by Jason Pontin, "Nanotechnology: The real fantastic voyage," *Red Herring,* July 2, 2001, www.redherring.com/mag/issue99/810019681.html.

page 14: "The Nanotech Report," a study: Josh Wolfe, "The Nanotech Report," August 2001.

page 16: By 2005, the $100 billion computer-memory: S. Sundar, "Magnoelectronics in Nanotechnology," *Techkriti Newsletter,* March 1, 2001.

page 16: The scientific breakthrough of 2001: Robert F. Service, "Molecules Get Wired," *Science,* December 21, 2001, pp. 2,442–2,443.

page 17: In 2001, Toyota: Jonathon Fahey, "The Science of the Small," *Forbes,* February 5, 2001, p. 124.

page 17: In the words of Richard Feynman: Richard P. Feynman, "There's Plenty of Room at the Bottom," speech to the American Physical Science Society, December 29, 1959.

Chapter One

page 19: On November 9, 1989: Don Eigler, e-mail conversation with the authors, April 24, 2002. (The actual date Eigler and Schweizer first moved an atom was September 28, 1989. It was not, however, until November 9–10 that they constructed the now-famous IBM logo made of the xenon atoms.)

page 20: ask someone born in 1960: S. Moore and J. L. Simon, "The Greatest Century That Ever Was: 25 Miraculous Trends of the Past 100 Years," *Policy Analysis*, No. 364, December 15, 1999. (www.cato.org/pubs/pas/pa364.pdf)

page 24: Figure 1.1 reprinted from I. Amato, "Nanotechnology: Shaping the World Atom by Atom" (a brochure for the public), 1999, page 3.

page 28: In the words of Horst Stormer: Jack Uldrich, "State needs to get involved in nanotechnology," *The Business Journal,* May 28, 2001.

page 35: "The principles of physics . . .": Richard P. Feynman, "There's Plenty of Room at the Bottom," speech to the American Physical Science Society, December 29, 1959.

page 35: "The problems of chemistry and biology . . .": ibid.

page 37: Granted, a snowball: Richard Siegel, "Creating Nanoplace Materials," *Scientific American,* December 1996, p. 74.

page 40: A 1999 report issued by the World Technology Evaluation Center: M. C. Roco, R. S. Williams, and P. Alivisatos, *Nanotechnology Research Directions: IWGN Workshop Report,* Kluwer Academic Publishers, 2000.

Chapter Two

page 44: Although both companies are involved: NNI Regional Symposium, Rice University, Houston, TX, May 23, 2002.

page 49: For example in Minnesota there are at least six corporations: These companies include Medtronic Inc., MTS Test Systems, Seagate Technologies, 3M, Honeywell Inc., Ecolab, General Dynamics, and others. This information was provided in a University of Minnesota report on Minnesota Center for Applied Nanoscience (now OMNI).

page 54: According to *MIT Technology Review*: Alexandra Stikeman, "Nanobiotech Makes the Diagnosis," *MIT Technology Review*, May 2002, page 66.

Chapter Three

page 67: "It is widely recognized . . .": Greg Orwig, "Center for Nanotechnology Has Big Plans for the Super Small," *University Week*, University of Washington, vol. 15, no. 14, January 29, 1998 (http://depts.washington.edu/uweek/archives/1998.01.JAN_29/article1.html).

page 67: "The total societal impact . . .": M. C. Roco, R. S. Williams, and P. Alivisatos, *Nanotechnology Research Directions: IWGN Workshop Report,* Kluwer Academic Publishers, 2000, p. xxxii.

page 67: that led President Clinton to fund: www.nano.gov.

page 68: not alone in its efforts to develop nanotechnology: P. Holister and T. Harper, *The Nanotechnology Opportunity Report,* CMP-Científica, 2002.

page 68: And working with all of these agencies: Candace Stuart, "Nanotexas: The Land of Big Oil Is Now Boomtown for the Tiny," *Small Times,* July 16, 2001.

page 69: In 2001, California and New York both kicked off: J. Uldrich, "State Needs to Get Involved in Nanotechnology," *Business Journal,* May 28, 2001.

page 69: In the case of California: Kelly Hearn, "Regions Across the Nation Vie for Nanotech Capital Title," www.smalltimes.com, July 16, 2001.

page 69: New York's $50 million program: ibid.

page 69: According to Michael Cox: Philip E. Ross, "The Road to Lilliput," *Red Herring,* June 15 & July 1, 2001, p. 48.

page 71: Progress, however, is not limited: A. Machlis, "Hebrew University Joins Israeli Push Toward NanoResearch with $40 Million Center," www.smalltimes.com, June 21, 2001.

page 72: Israeli researchers claim: A. Machlis, "Israel's Big Science, VC Sectors Are 'Just Waking Up' to Nanotech," www.smalltimes. com, December 10, 2001.

page 72: the cost of a gram of single-walled carbon tubes: "Cost-Effective Controlled Production of Single-Walled Carbon Nano-tubes," W. E. Alvarez, L. Balzano, J. E. Herrera, and D. E. Resasco, School of Chemical Engineering and Materials Science, University of Oklahoma. www.ou.edu/engineering/nanotube/NT2001Production. PDF.

page 73: it costs NASA $10,000 to launch: D. Polkill, "Space: The Ultimate Price," Independence Institute, November 17, 1999. www. i2i.org.

page 75: Elan Pharmaceutical has publicly stated: P. McGee, "Nanotech Valley?," www.technophilly.com, Vol. 1, Issue 12 (www. technophilly.com/NEWS/N-0112-nano.html).

page 75: Advectus Life Sciences claims: "Advectus to Test Nano-Based Treatment for Brain Tumors," www.smalltimes.com, May 31, 2002.

page 76: According to one National Science Foundation official: Edmund Wong, assistant director of the National Science Foundation for Engineering, "Nanoscale Science and Technology: Opportunities for the Twenty-First Century," Subcommittee on Basic Research, June 22, 1999.

page 77: Altair Nanotechnologies, another publicly traded company: Nanotechnology stocks are extremely risky and are vulnerable to hype. Readers who are interested in investing in nanotechnology are encouraged to do their due diligence. Currently there are two publi-cations, the "Forbes/Wolfe Nanotech Report" and the "X Report," published by CMP-Científica, that offer sound information on the emerging nanotechnology-investment market.

page 77: By the end of 2003: Mark Calvey, "Jurvetson pins big hopes on tiny nanomachines," *San Francisco Business Times,* July 13, 2001.

page 78: Ardesta LLC is also aggressively: www.crainsdetroit.com

page 81: The memory market is a $100 billion annual: S. Sundar, "Magnoelectronics in Nanotechnology," *Techkriti Newsletter,* March 1, 2001.

Chapter Four

page 88: Since 1988, the price of storing one megabyte: P. Meyer, "What's Going On?," www.zonezero.com, October 2002 (www.zonezero.com/editorial/octubre00/october.html)

page 93: Corrosion is estimated to cost U.S. businesses: "Corrosion Research Reaps Reward," *Deseret News*, November 27, 2000.

page 93: Considering that the Navy spends $75,000 a day: "Shortage of Cash for Fuel Leaves Navy Ships Parked at Pier," *Stars and Stripes*, August 28, 2000.

page 93: 98 percent of world trade: www.shreyas.com/shippingintro.htm.

page 96: In tests, the material: Linda Wang, "Paving Out Pollution: A Common Whitener Helps to Clean the Air," *Scientific American,* February 23, 2002.

page 96: a thirtyfold increase in the combustion rate in solid rockets: www.technanogy.net.

page 97: responsible for close to $1 billion in sales: American Home Products' 2001 Annual Report.

page 98: market for acne products: "Dermatological Pharmaceuticals" (Table), Medical and Healthcare Marketplace Guide—1998, Copyright © 1998 by Dorlands Directories.

page 98: mouthwash industry: U.S. Sales of Mouthwashes/Dental Rinses (1996–2000), Table 3.696, Consumer, U.S.A. 2002, 6th edition, Euromonitor Plc, London.

page 103: NASA, which currently spends between: D. Polkill, "Space: The Ultimate Price," Independence Institute, November 17, 1999, www.i2i.org/publications/op-eds/politicsandgovernment/space.

page 103: This might sound unlikely, but: www.hitachi-hri.com/english.

Chapter Five

page 106: Understanding how proteins fold: researchweb.watson.ibm.com/bluegene/protein_folding.html.

page 107: 17,000 nursing homes: "Special Investigation: Nursing Homes," United States House of Representatives Committee on Government Reform Minority Office, May 2002 (www.house.gov/reform/min/inves_nursing/).

page 107: 76 million baby-boomers: www.bbhq.com/whatsabm.htm.

page 107: $600 billion long-term care industry: AARP: American Association of Retired People, www.research.aarp.org/health/fs10r_nursing.html.

page 108: Nanosphere, a company located: Kristin Philpkoski, "Instant Diagnosis in Your Palm," *Wired News,* February 21, 2002.

page 110: salmonella (which affects an estimated: "Customers That Gag on Cost of Technology Should Find a Business Solution More Palatable," J. Pepper, www.smalltimes.com, June 6, 2001.

page 110: For example, Michael Tailor: Richard Acello, "Tiny Chips Squeeze into Tight Spots, Serving as Scouts in War and Peace," www.smalltimes.com, November 28, 2001.

page 110: California's $6.8 billion wine industry: "The Day California Wine Came of Age," *BusinessWeek* Online, May 8, 2001 (www.businessweek.com/bwdaily/dnflash/may2001/nf2001058_228.htm).

page 112: Once the attachment between protein and cancer cell: "Tiny 'Smart Bombs' can invade, kill cancer," www.CNN.com, November 15, 2001.

page 112: Preliminary tests have shown that this smart bomb: "A 'Smart-Bomb' That Cures," CBSNews.com, November 15, 2001 (www.cbsnews.com/stories/2001/11/15/health/main318216.shtml).

page 114: A new nanoscale device: Richard Acello, "Aerosol Drug Delivery System Boosted by 'Little Whiffle Balls,'" www.smalltimes.com, December 28, 2001.

page 114: Quantum Dot Corporation: Stephan Herrera, "Doctor's Little Helpers," *Red Herring,* June 15 & July 1, 2001, p. 52.

page 114: completely disrupt the $2.8 billion fluorescent tagging market: D. Rotman, "Quantum Dot Com," *Technology Review,* January/February 2000.

page 115: Today's car engines: Alan Leo, "Fuel cells in brief," *Technology Review,* February 5, 2002.

page 116: Ford, Daimler-Chrysler, and Volkswagen are all also placing: "Hydrogen: 'Petroleum' of the Future?," *EcoWatch,* Worldwatch Institute, October 12, 2001.

page 118: $10 billion battery industry: Ann Chambers, "Battery Market to Top $10B by 2003: Survey," *Power Engineering Magazine,* July 1999—Forecasting a $10.8 billion market in 2003.

page 119: From a minuscule $1.5 million: P. Holister and T. Harper, *The Nanotechnology Opportunity Report,* CMP-Científica, 2002.

page 119: Resasco reported in late 2001: "Oklahoma chemist says he's unlocked secret to faster nanotube production," *The Oklahoman,* December 26, 2001.

page 119: Another company: Miwako Waga, "Japanese Companies Getting Ready to Churn Out Nanotubes by the Ton," www.smalltimes.com, March 13, 2002.

page 121: diesel vehicles in California spew 28,000 tons: R. Clandos,

"New Nanotechnology Applications Will Help Snuff Out Smog by Cleaning Dirty Diesel," www.smalltimes.com, July 12, 2001.

page 121: A Johns Hopkins study has even estimated that: "Independent Analysis Affirms Soot Particles Are Deadly, Lung Association Notes," www.lungusa.org/press/envir/air_062800.html.

page 121: Engelhard Corporation: Rosemary Clandos, "New Nanotechnology Applications Will Help Snuff Out Smog by Cleaning Dirty Diesel," www.smalltimes.com, July 12, 2001.

page 122: With an estimated 15 percent of wells: ibid.

page 122: The product may also: ibid

page 122: Argonide Corporation: Jeffrey M. Perkel, "Nanotech Dream," *The Scientist,* March 4, 2002.

page 123: Now picture that superhighway: David J. Bishop, C. Randy Giles, and Saswato R. Das, "The Rise of Optical Switching," *Scientific American,* January 2001.

page 124: $550 billion telecommunications industry: *Plunkett's Telecommunication Industry Almanac 2001–2002.*

Chapter Six

page 127: And in a move: Richard Martin, "Meltdown: On October 15 Big Steel Became a Museum," *Wired,* February 10, 2002.

page 128: $139 billion semiconductor industry: Semiconductor Industry Association (2001).

page 130: Motorola is already working: Ivan Amato, "Motorola's Superchip," Technology Review, April 2002.

page 130: will have developed a series of chips: ibid.

page 132: electronic paper is going to require the $60 billion newspaper, the $59 billion periodical, and the $23 billion book publishing industries to rethink their business models: www.bizstats.com/marketsizes.htm.

page 133: $108 billion U.S. printing industry: ibid.

page 135: $85 billion advertising industry: ibid.

page 140: By 2006, it is estimated that: B. Whitmore, "German Company Envisions Giant Freight Airships," *Boston Globe*, February 3, 2001.

page 143: $181 billion apparel industry: www.bizstats.com/marketsizes. htm.

page 143: 376,000 firefighters: Statistical Abstract of the U.S. 2001 National Data Book, U.S. Department of Commerce. Information as of March 1999.

page 144: 200,000 pharmacists: ibid.

page 145: $13 billion chocolate market: Sales of Chocolate Confectionery (1996–2000), Table 3.260, Consumer, U.S.A. 2002, 6th Edition, Euromonitor Plc, London.

page 145: An Israeli company, Nutralease: Avi Machlis, "Health-care Ingredients Hitch Ride in Nanovehicle for Direct Delivery," www.smalltimes.com, January 31, 2002.

page 146: Over the next thirty years, the U.S. government is: "New Technology Revolutionizing Ground Water Clean-Up," www.ewire-news.com. Source: Lehigh University.

page 146: The previous best: "New Technology Revolutionizing Ground Water Clean-Up," Hoover's Online, www.lehigh.edu, March 13, 2002.

page 147: Researchers at Lehigh University: ibid.

Chapter Seven

page 152: In a study with rats: A. Gagnon and A. Sovisky, "The Effect of Glucose Concentration on Insulin-Induced 3T3-L1 Adysose Cell Differentiation," *Obesity Research,* November 2, 2001.

page 152: In one study: Alan I. Leshner, "We Can Conquer Drug Addiction," *The Futurist,* November 1999.

page 153: One of the most promising applications: "Nanotechnology in Biology: The Good of Small Things," *The Economist,* December 12, 2001.

page 155: Throughout the twentieth century, cancer was: T. Henderson, "Patients Will Demand Better, Faster Diagnoses and Treatments, Docs Say," www.smalltimes.com, September 26, 2001.

page 160: Currently $80 billion worth of plant oil: *The Futurist,* December 1999.

page 161: today's best solar cells convert: B. Sanders, "Cheap, Plastic Solar Cells May Be on the Horizon, Thanks to New Technology Developed by UC Berkeley, LBNL Chemists," Berkeley Press Release, March 28, 2002 (www.berkeley.edu/news/media/releases/2002/03/28_solar.html).

page 162: This will represent a savings: www.nano.gov.

Chapter Eight

page 167: Nanotechnology-enabled solar cells: "Cheap, plastic solar cells may be on the horizon, thanks to new technology developed by UC Berkeley, LBNL chemists," *UC Berkeley Campus News,* March 29, 2002.

page 171: The waiting list for people desiring an organ: "Cloned Pigs May Offer Human Transplant Organs," www.msnbc.com/news, August 22, 2002.

page 172: Extracting existing chromosomes: Robert Freitas, www.KurzweilAl.net, February 26, 2002.

page 173: Neurons could be encapsulated: ibid.

page 173: The sphere, likely a tailor-made nanomaterial: ibid.

page 176: The United Nations estimates: National Intelligence Council, "Global Trends 2015" (http://www.cia.gov/cia/publications/globaltrends2015/).

page 177: If such predictions seem to stretch credibility: S. Moore and J. L. Simon, "The Greatest Century That Ever Was: 25 Miraculous Trends of the Past 100 Years." Policy Analysis, No. 364, December 15, 1999 (www.cato.org/pubs/pas/pa364.pdf).

page 178: The second and more fundamental problem: Richard E. Smalley, "Of Chemistry, Love and Nanobots," *Scientific American,* September 2001.

page 179: The third and final problem: ibid.

Chapter Nine

page 187: A survey of nanotechnology experts: M. C. Roco, R. S. Williams, and P. Alivisatos. *Nanotechnology Research Directions: IWGN Workshop Report,* Kluwer Academic Publishers, 2000, p. xli.

RESOURCES

News Sources

www.nanoveritas.com: A comprehensive nanotechnology website dedicated to providing the general business reader with relevant nanotechnology news. The site is produced and maintained by Jack Uldrich and Deb Newberry, the authors of *The Next Big Thing Is Really Small: How Nanotechnology Will Change the Future of Your Business.*

www.smalltimes.com: A daily news site covering nanotechnology developments.

www.nanotech-now.com: A website that posts links to a variety of nanotechnology articles.

www.foresight.org: The leading think tank on nanotechnology. The organization is dedicated to advancing the development of nanotechnology and committed to sharing information in order to promote sound private and public-policy decisions.

www.nanobusiness.org: A trade association developed to promote the nanotechnology industry.

www.nanotechplanet.com: A website that profiles emerging nanotechnology companies and key leaders in the industry.

Books

M. C. Roco, R. S. Williams, and P. Alivisatos, *Nanotechnology Research Directions: IWGN Workshop Report,* Kluwer Academic Publishers, 2000.

Nanotechnology: Shaping the World Atom by Atom, National Science and Technology Council Committee on Technology, September 1999.

B. C. Crandall and J. Lewis, *Nanotechnology: Research and Perspectives,* MIT Press, Cambridge, 1992.

K. E. Drexler, *Engines of Creation: The Coming Era of Nanotechnology,* Anchor Books, New York, 1986.

Government Resources

The National Nanotechnology Initiative:

www.nano.gov

Six U.S. Centers of Excellence:

1. Center for Integrated Nanopatterning and Detection Technologies: Northwestern University: **www.nsec.northwestern.edu**

2. Center for Nanoscale Systems in Information Technologies, Cornell University: **www.cns.cornell.edu**

3. Center for Science of Nanoscale Systems and their Device Applications, Harvard: **www.nsec.harvard.edu**

4. Center for Electronic Transport in Molecular Nanostructures, Columbia: **www.cise.columbia.edu/nsec**

5. Center for Nanoscience in Biological and Environmental Engineering, Rice University: **www.ruf.rice.edu**

6. Center for Directed Assembly of Nanostructures, Rensselaer: **www.rpi.edu/dept/research/nanotech_abstract1.html**

The Institute of Nanotechnology:

www.nano.org/uk

ACKNOWLEDGMENTS

We want to first thank our families for the patience they have demonstrated and the support they have provided for us while we were writing this book. We especially want to thank our spouses, Cindy and Jerry, who have had to shoulder more than their fair share of the parenting responsibilities as we strived to finish the book. We also want to thank our literary agent, Greg Dinkin, and his partner, Frank Scatoni, for believing that the topic of nanotechnology warranted publication . . . and John Mahaney of Crown Business for agreeing. Our editor at Crown Business, Shana Wingert, deserves immense praise for constantly pushing us to make the topic of nanotechnology more manageable (and digestible) for the reader. As a result of her tireless efforts, the book is significantly better. We also want to thank our readers and reviewers, David Kennan, Paul Gourley, Steve Vetter, Paul Wendorff, Steve Jurvetson, Hank Lederer, and Philip Kuekes for their time, insight, and constructive criticism. The book is much stronger as a result of their willingness to so freely share their knowledge and expertise. Finally, thanks are due to the many men and women who contributed directly and indirectly to the substance of this book, especially the pioneers in the field of nanotechnology . . . you are the people who are making it happen.

INDEX

chemistry, supramolecular, 38
Chevron Technology, 78–79
China, 68, 72
cholesterol, 16, 145
chromosome-replacement therapy, 172–73
circuits, molecular, 16, 26–27
Clinton, Bill, 67
clothing industry
chip-embedded clothing, 168
fashion design and, 142–43
protective clothing, 69, 120,
142–43
stain-resistant clothing, 15, 99
CMP Científica, 78
Columbia University, 71
communications industry, 123–25
competition, business, 51–52,
59–60
computer industry. *See also* semiconductor industry
carbon nanotubes and, 137–38
computing power in, 30, 39,
174–76
data storage and, 85–88
law of computing power in, 21,
128
stronger batteries and, 118
computing, distributed, 39
construction materials, 90, 95,
143–44
consultants, hiring of, 50–51
consumer behavior, 183–85
contact lens manufacturers, 96
copier market, 91
Cornell University, 71
corporations, 13, 43–65
allocating R&D dollars, 52–60
assessing competition, 51–52
consultants for, 50–51
employee incentives, 46–47
employee recruiting, 47–51
long-range strategic goals,
60–62
manufacturing processes, 63–64
quality control processes, 63–64
R&D spinoffs from, 62
strategic planning, 60–62

university partners for, 49–50,
53–55
corrosion-resistant coatings,
92–93
cosmetics industry, 30, 97, 98
CritiTech, Inc., 113
cyanide, 147

Daimler-Chrysler, 76, 116
data-storage devices, 85–88
De Forest, Lee, 164
Defense Department, 139
defense industry, 68–69
dendrimers, 153
Department of Energy, 68
Department of Transportation, 68
depression, 16–17, 33
Desai, Tejal, 113
diabetes, 32, 113, 185–86
diet industry, 144–46, 152
disease. *See also specific diseases*
diagnosing, 106, 107–11
genetic nature of, 152
molecular nature of, 33
disk-drive market, 85–88
disruptive technology, 27–28, 78
distributed computing, 39
DNA markers, 107
drug abuse and addiction, 152–53
drug-delivery systems
implantable devices, 32,
56–58, 111–13, 144, 186
nanocrystals, 113–14
nanotags, 114
skin patches, 185
smart bombs, 112–13
Duke University, 70
DuPont, 94

ecosystem, 137–38
Eddie Bauer, 15, 99
education, 133–34, 187
Eigler, Don, 19–20
Elan Pharmaceutical, 75
electric industry, 117
electronic paper, 132–34
electronics industry, 16, 30, 187
Eli Lilly, 17, 75

self-assembly, 26, 35
semiconductor industry
    plastic chips in, 131–36
    silicon chips in, 26–27, 128–29
    super chips in, 129–31, 135–36
sensors, 108–11, 155–60
Sequenom, 69
silicon chips, 26–27, 128–29
Singapore, 136
ski industry, 90–91
skin, growing, 171
Smalley, Richard, 14, 40, 79
smallpox, 109
smalltimes.com, 78
solar-cell technology, 161,
    167–68
South Korea, 68
space exploration. *See* NASA
spectrometer, 37
Stanford University, 54, 70
steel industry, 29, 127–28
"sticky fingers" problem, 179
stockbrokers, 175
strategic planning, 60–62
"Striction," 179
Sun Microsystems, 69
SuNyx, 91
super chips, 129–31, 135–36
supramolecular chemistry, 38
SurroMed, 109
SWNTs, 119

tagging, 114
Tailor, Michael, 110
Taiwan, 68
Technanogy, 96
telecommunications industry,
    123–25
telomerase, 172
terrorism, 110
Texas, 70
TheraFuse, Inc., 32
thermoelectric energy, 162
third-world countries, 176–77
titanium dioxide nanoparticles,
    94–96

tobacco industry, 152–53
Toray Industries, 74
Toto, Ltd., 95
toy industry, 92
Toyota Corporation, 17, 76, 102,
    116
Trane, 146
transportation industry
    computer-operated vehicles in,
        169
    corrosion-resistant materials in,
        93
    fuel calculations in, 87
    fuel efficiency and, 103
    nanomaterials in, 120, 140
    weather forecasting for, 137
travel industry, 27, 137

universities
    corporate partners for, 49–50,
        53–55
    curriculum changes in, 87
    nanotechnology centers at, 13,
        70–72
U.S. Air Force, 92
U.S. Army, 69, 141–43
U.S. Navy, 92–93, 139–40

vaccines, 160–61
Veeco Instruments, 77
venture capitalists, 13, 77–79
vinyl flooring, 90
viruses, 33, 36, 111, 112
Volkswagen, 76, 116

water shortages, 176
water-treatment plants, 146
weather forecasting, 137
Wilson Sporting Goods, 101
windows, self-cleaning, 91–92
wine industry, 110–11, 159–60

Xerox, 91

ZettaCore, 27, 82, 88
Zyvex Corporation, 82, 179

ABOUT THE AUTHORS

JACK ULDRICH is president of The NanoVeritas Group, a consultancy that focuses on helping businesses, venture capitalists, and governments understand and profit from nanotechnology. From 1999 to 2002, he served as the deputy director of the Office of Strategic and Long Range Planning for the state of Minnesota and has written and spoken widely on the subject of nanotechnology. He is a former naval intelligence officer and served as a policy analyst for the Department of Defense. Uldrich is also a senior associate of the Foresight Institute and a charter member of the NanoBusiness Alliance. Uldrich lives in Minneapolis, Minnesota, with his wife, Cindy, and their two children.

DEB NEWBERRY is a business consultant and nuclear physicist with a broad technical background, who has more than twenty-three years experience in research, technology management, and corporate leadership positions. She has authored a number of technical papers and served in national leadership positions within the Institute of Electrical and Electronics Engineers and the Aerospace Industries Association. Newberry is currently consulting with multiple companies to determine how emerging technologies will impact their products and markets, how to optimize investments, and how to leverage technical advancements. She is also chairman of the board of directors for Project Universe, a nonprofit that provides education and public outreach in science and math. Newberry lives in Burnsville, Minnesota, with her husband, Jerry, and their three children.